The many faces of France

Th

Texts by Pierre Leprohon

MINERVA

many faces of France

Texts translated by Blanche Michaëls

Contents

Title pages: View of Auvers-sur-Oise.

PRINTED IN ITALY BY ISTITUTO ITALIANO D'ARTI GRAFICHE - BERGAMO

© *Editions Minerva S.A., Genève, 1974.*
Printed in Italy. ISBN 0-8148-0580-9

Library of Congress Cataloging in Publication Data

Leprohon, Pierre.
    The many faces of France.

ABOUT FRANCE

If we are to understand France, we must first place it, geographically and historically.

On a planisphere where the two giant continents, Eurasia and America, are projected, France occupies a central position in Western Europe—the central position from East to West and from North to South, between Arctic circle and Equator, between ice and sun, cold and hot.

Thus it is a well-balanced land, refusing extremes. But the central point that it occupies is also a frontier between the two elements that make up our planet: land and water, the Eurasian continent to the east and the ocean to the west, aridity and moisture, fixity and motion.

France's climate and character alike are temperate. The reputed "furia francese" is promptly calmed by good sense.

Equilibrium and proportion. These are not clichés. One has only to look at an Ile de France landscape or at life in a provincial town.

That is what the country looks like from the outside. Let us go closer; let us go into it and see that this "balanced union" is made up of diversity and contrasts.

France is indeed a land of encounter. As we get to know it the environmental characteristics do not fade away abruptly but reveal themselves and are welded together. The central plateau, prehistoric country, marks the point of contact. To the north, climate, race and features are those of the Celtic and Anglo-Saxon worlds while to the south they are Greco-Latin. In the north

The "hamlet" of Versailles.

A farm on the Ile-de-France. Right: The "Route Napoléon" in the Alps.

grow the beech and the birch, in the south the cypress and the olive.

If France has a very definite entity, it is also the most varied country in Europe, the least like itself in its component parts.

To a great extent its geographical position has also influenced its history. Located at the extreme tip of Europe, with its back to the immense Atlantic Ocean, France constituted the last bastion and has seen successive waves of every invasion break on its shores, invasions from every quarter: Normans from the north, Germans and Mongols from the west and Romans and Arabs from the south. The country has endured these intrusions but it has also broken and hurled them back. Even more cleverly it has assimilated the invaders, accepting their culture and what they had to give.

France is a country with a mind open to ideas, which it transforms and makes its own. France never surrounded itself in racial or political autarchy. Because it practices an open door policy, it has earned a reputation as a land of liberty.

In the spheres of knowledge and tourism, France's diversity, its instinctive appeal on contact, charm the foreigner, sure of meeting neither hostility nor boredom. Each region has its own special character, each province its own quality. Its contour is like its seas, made up of different aspects but always attuned to man: from the endless beaches of the North Sea to the rocks of Brittany and the coves of Provence; from the peaceful hills of Normandy to the "rounded mountain tops" of Alsace and the glaciers of the Alps...

Everywhere in this countryside history has left its mark, in the castles and churches like so many hands placed on the mantle of time.

Poets have called it "la doulce France"... In spite of the century in which we live, it still deserves that name.

Pierre Leprohon

1 - THE PARISIAN BASIN AND THE SEINE VALLEY

Aside from its location, France's extreme centralization characterizes it among Western European countries.

Down through the centuries all the routes of communication, all activities having to do with the marketing of goods and all the expressions of its spirit and its genius have converged on France's capital, located in the approximate heart of the country.

The roads of France and its railway system start from Paris and end there. Because of its rivers and its extensive system of canals, the Parisian region is also at the center of the waterways.

France thus appears to be an enormous spider's web—or better still a star with radiating points.

The Parisian basin was well-qualified to become a capital since it is out of the way of the mountain ranges, is easily reached by its plains and its rivers and is not far from the sea, to which it is linked by the Seine.

What nature favored has been improved by the work of man and, especially since the 19th century, Paris has become the magnet that attracts the molecules.

Today the Parisian agglomeration consists of more than 7,000,000 inhabitants out of a population of 50,000,000 for the whole country. This means that one out of every seven Frenchmen lives or works in this Greater Paris—sometimes threatened with asphyxiation.

For the economy and the towns such a concentration creates difficulties for the State. It has tried to reduce these problems by decentralization (which however conflicts with other vital demands) and by trying to spread the population along a kind of diagonal running north towards the sea, Rouen and Le Havre and south towards Orléans.

The creation of satellite-cities was a solution that would make it possible for the capital and its environs to keep their age-old quality and the charm so greatly threatened by the population explosion, for in France, as elsewhere, it is now realized that man does not live by his activity and work alone but perhaps first and foremost by the physical and spiritual climate that surrounds him.

Left: The castle of Champs.
Below: The Valley of the Oise.

Paris, the heart of France

Ancient Lutetia.

The history of Paris is that of the embryo, the seed. This important village was born on the islands of the Sequana (Seine) whose loops enclosed marshy lands. It was called "Lutetia", which means marsh. Caesar was the first to mention it in his *Commentaries.*

The "Pax Romana" which followed the conquest led to an initial development on the Left Bank but the invasions of the Barbarians confined the city to the islands. Referring to Lutetia in 358, the Emperor Julian wrote: "It is the name given by the Celts to the small town of the Parisians (Parisii) located on the river which surrounds it on all sides. It is connected with both banks by two wooden bridges."

Examination of an historic map of the city shows that the original nucleus developed by concentric waves like sapwood in the growth of a tree. Ile de la Cité kept its name although, towards the 10th century, the first surrounding wall dating from the Capetians went beyond those banks into farmlands and inhabited lands that are called *clos.*

The city expanded under Philip Augustus, and churches, palaces, convents and covered markets were built. To the north Paris already reached what are today called the Grands Boulevards and to the south it went as far as St. Germain.

At the end of the 18th century the wall called the Fermiers Généraux enclosed the faubourgs of St.Antoine, Montmartre, the Temple, etc. Fifty years later (1841-1845) a new line of ramparts and gates took in the free towns of Charonne, Belleville, Montmartre, Passy, Auteuil and Vaugirard. This wall is situated approximately on the site of what has become the Peripheral Boulevard. Thus time here defines space.

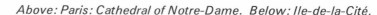

Above: Paris: Cathedral of Notre-Dame. Below: Ile-de-la-Cité.

Perhaps the most beautiful urban vista in the world: the Tuileries gardens, the obelisk of the Place de la Concorde, the Arc de Triomphe.

Ile de la Cité.

This huge city is one of the most compact imaginable. Paris does not have the breathing space that is provided, for example, by Rome's ruins, London's parks or Berlin's forests. Green spaces surround it but the heart of the city is a human anthill through which the lazy Seine meanders with indolent nonchalance.

Nevertheless, in spite of this coming together of the centuries and modern life, each "section" of Paris retains its character and appearance. This is the charm of Paris for those who know the city and for the curious traveler who will have the pleasure of discovering it.

The best way to make this discovery is still to follow the thread of history down the ages crossing the bridges to reach the Ile de la Cité opposite Notre-Dame, whose massive towers rise with a grace that is due to the buoyancy of the buttresses. Notre-Dame de Paris! Faith, art, history, everything is there under the sublime vaults that are prayer and witness alike.

Surrounding it, encircled by the arms of the Seine, the visual symphony sounds its first strains: stone, water, greenness. Parks may be rare in Paris, but trees are everywhere, the fragile mobility of their foliage contrasting with the austerity of the old stones: along the quays, on the avenues and in the small squares where children play or lovers dream.

Set between the arms of the river, Ile de la Cité could be a ship whose high mast was Notre-Dame, with the tip of Vert-Gallant as its prow and the apse of the cathedral as its stern.

Many faces...

The Parisian and, perhaps even more, the foreigner think of Paris as the "Left Bank" and most especially the Latin Quarter. This is the uncontested territory of the intellectuals, the booksellers, the publishers and above all the university and high school students who, since the Middle Ages, have made it the most turbulent section of Paris.

It is the domain of the old schools of the Sorbonne, of narrow streets with cosmopolitan restaurants, of the Luxembourg Garden and of those cafés where so many famous names have left their imprint for all time. It is here that one must breathe the spirit of Paris, so communicative that it has made its very own many, so many intellects from far and wide.

The jewels of the Left Bank are the Sainte-Chapelle and Sainte-Geneviève; its memorials are the Conciergerie, the Panthéon and even, there also, the well-known cafés such as Procope, the oldest in Paris, where politicians philosophers, artists and poets meet.

But to be acquainted with the ostentation of the old regime, one must go to the Ile Saint-Louis which is a continuation of the Ile de la Cité. Along its old quays rise, in all their severe beauty, the mansions of Louis XIV's time: Lambert, Astry, Lauzun, Jassaud and many others where, after the noblemen, 19th century painters and scholars lived.

Châtelet, the Bastille, the Hôtel de Ville and the Marais on the right bank are also the Paris of History, rich in ghosts and monuments from the past. There too, especially in the Marais, one finds marvelous 17th and 18th century mansions, in side-streets that are often sordid.

The Eiffel Tower and the Paris of modern times.

The great Parisian axis.

In the capital's concentric development it is curious to note the thrust to the west that is typical of population expansion everywhere. While the artisans of the Faubourg St.Antoine, the wine merchants of Bercy and warehouses of all kinds settled behind the islands, it was towards the prow, the front of the Cité, that there took shape the wonderful vista which stretches from the Tuileries to the Etoile and then to the Defense, down the city's magisterial highway. The rue de Rivoli and its arcades, the Louvre's sumptuous façades, the privileged enclosure of the Palais Royal and the cool gardens of the Tuileries lead to the Place de la Concorde, that vast amphitheater of Parisian life. It is the prelude to the Champs-Elysées and to the avenues leading to the Arc de Triomphe de l'Etoile which radiates out towards the Paris of elegance, business and tourism.

This axis pierces like an arrow the successive walls with which history has tried to encircle the city. Everything around it is within easy reach: the Grand Palais, the Champs-de-Mars, the Invalides, the Eiffel Tower, the Opera and the Grands Boulevards, the commercial nerve center.

But in order to know Paris, one must also travel around it between the walls that have successively fixed its limits. The "villages" are there: Auteuil and Passy, refuge of the old bourgeoisie, Grenelle and Vaugirard, disturbed by

buildings of the year 2000, and Montparnasse and St.Germain-des-Prés with their literary cafés and their nightclubs. To the east are Bercy, still dedicated to the god Bacchus, and Charonne and Belleville, where the earthy vigor that produces variety singers

and "gamins" lives on. Finally comes Montmartre which manages to retain its charm in spite of tourists and "shady characters". It is always the Montmartre so greatly loved by those who have sung its praises with pen or paintbrush.

Above: The clock of the Palais de Justice. Right: The famous church of St.-Germain-des-Prés.

Contrasts... the quays along the Seine, the vault of the church of St.-Sulpice, modern buildings along the Seine.

"Paris by night". Champs-Ely-sées, Place de la Concorde, Palais de Chaillot.

Everyone knows that Paris is one of the world's biggest centers of "objets d'art". *Below: Window of an antique shop. Facing page: Old capital portraying the celebrated lovers Héloïse and Abélard. Right: Door of an old baker's shop.*

Héloïse and Abélard: theirs is the most moving and the most tragic of love stories. Born towards the end of the 11th century, Pierre Abélard was at 25 one of the most subtle dialecticians of the Parisian School. He was at the height of his glory and his disciples were flocking from all parts of Europe to hear his theological arguments when he fell passionately in love with one of his pupils, the niece of Canon Fulbert.

Héloïse became his mistress and gave birth to a boy. The angered Canon hired men to subject Abélard to that most infamous of mutilations—castration. Abélard then retired to the Abbey of Saint-Denis while Héloïse entered the convent of Argenteuil. Soon, however, his disciples begged Abélard to resume his public teaching, but his audacious views soon earned him the enmity of the Church. In 1122 the Synod of Soissons ordered that his *Introduction to Theology* be burned.

Discouraged, Abélard retired to the hermitage of Paraclet, then to the monastery of Saint-Gildas in Brittany and finally to the Priory of Saint-Marcel in the Saône, where he died in 1142. He can be considered as the founder of philosophy in the Middle Ages.

Héloïse, 20 years younger than Abélard, was more likely the daughter than the niece of the Canon whose odious vengeance aroused the indignation of his contemporaries. In spite of their vows and their separation, the passion of the two lovers could not die. That this was so is proved by their correspondence. Published later, it is moving testimony to a love that by far exceeded mere physical bonds.

Héloïse became Abbess of the Convent of Argenteuil and later settled with her nuns at Paraclet, placed at their disposal by Abélard. It is at Paraclet that the philosopher was buried. Twenty-two years later the body of Héloïse was placed besides his in the same tomb.

With Tristan and Isolde, they are the most famous of the lovers immortalized in French literature.

Gardens of the "Petit Trianon" at Versailles.

The Environs of Paris

Let us enlarge the circle. The Paris of today is Greater Paris; it too has its hundred faces. In the north, the industrial centers are Saint-Denis, Aubervilliers, Bobigny and Le Bourget. To the east, on the banks of the Seine and the Marne, the small pavilions and pleasure gardens of days gone by are still there. To the south the industry that feeds supplies to the metropolis is being built up. Around Versailles, the west still clings to the marks of its former grandeur.

For history too is present and, like so many gems, the castles ornament this splendid crown of suburban cities. Versailles is the richest of these jewels. Starting from what was a pied-à-terre for Louis XIII, Louis XIV had the architect Le Vau and later Hardouin-Mansard create the prestigious whole whose nobility and balanced perfection have aroused the world's admiration. Le Nôtre designed the gardens with their ornamental lakes and fountains. The Orangerie and the Trianons add grace to the grandeur and help to make Versailles the finest expression of the French classical spirit.

Revolutions and wars have destroyed several castles which surrounded Paris: Marly, also built by Louis XIV, was razed to the ground at the time of the Revolution, St. Cloud and Sceaux, the latter being rebuilt in 1856. But although the estates have gone, the parks remain as havens of peace, like the woods that still exist especially in the western and southern suburbs. There are the forests of Saint-Germain and Marly and the woods of Meudon, Chaville and Verrières.

Other castles deserve mention: Saint-Germain-en-Laye, which goes back to the 12th century, became Henry IV's favorite residence after it was transformed and enlarged. Louis XIII died there and Louis XIV was born there. Today the castle houses the unusual Museum of National Antiques.

In Rueil the story of Napoleon and Josephine de Beauharnais comes alive at Malmaison, a charming residence in a verdant setting. The castle is now a museum to the memory of the Emperor and his Josephine.

Great Buildings and Pleasure Gardens

East of Paris, the castle of Vincennes is one of the most beautiful feudal domains in France. Built in the 14th century it was, before Versailles, the residence of the kings of France and a rendez-vous for hunters. The dungeon, surrounded by a turreted wall, is an impressive sight.

In the north the castles disappear. Here it is the basilica of Saint-Denis which attracts our attention. Within this first great Gothic structure are buried many of the kings and queens of France and thus it is a veritable museum of French funerary sculpture.

The former abbey next to it has become the museum of the Legion of Honor.

Historical associations always play a big role in the choice of sites to preserve. How many other sites have been destroyed by modern life? At the end of the last century the whole Seine Valley was the meeting place of the Impressionists and their succes-

sors: Monet and Renoir at Argenteuil, Seurat on the island of Grande-Jatte, and Van Gogh and Signac at Asnières. But now the green spaces have been replaced by factories and the sail boats by barges.

On the other side of Greater Paris, pleasure gardens are still to be found on the banks of the Marne where, on Sunday, couples go to dance and anglers drink their white wine: Nogent, Joinville, Le Perreux... It is a popular tradition, always dear to Parisians.

The Royal Crown

If the circle around the capital is extended even further the result is almost a province, the Ile-de-France, which appears as the nation's royal crown. In a new circle of gently rolling countryside and peaceful rivers it surrounds regions that used to be called "countries": Parisis, Vexin, Valois, Brie, Gâtinais, Hurepoix and even France itself—for before becoming a nation it consisted of several villages still known by their old names—Mareil-en-France, Roissy-en-France, etc.

The rivers which wind through these places meet again in the provinces: the Seine, the Oise, the Marne and the Eure. With the forests they are the characteristic feature of this area, rich in history. Here once again castles,

Left: The castle of Chantilly, its gardens and ornamental lakes. Above: The staircase of the castle of Fontainebleau.

cathedrals and old cities form a kind of garland around the capital, alternating with the forests of Fontainebleau, Rambouillet, Chantilly, Ermenonville, Compiègne, etc.

Each one of these places, each one of these residences is an enchantment to the senses, a feast for the spirit. No where else has the work of man blended better with nature. It is as a pilgrim of the past as well as a tourist that one should travel through the Ile-de-France.

Castles and Forests

Fontainebleau is castle and forest at one and the same time. Through the years the castle has known many changes but the essence of its beautiful Renaissance decoration was the work of Francis I. Italian artists were employed. Catherine de' Medici received princes and ambassadors there. Henry IV's son Louis XIII was born there. Louis XIV was much attached to Fontainebleau. In the castle's great hall of honor Napoleon took leave of his officers before going into exile.

The royal apartments, the drawing rooms, the galleries and the chapel contain innumerable treasures: furniture, paintings, and objects of all kinds. French and English gardens extend through the park.

The castle and the town are at the edge of forest, more than 6,500 acres, with a great wealth of pines, oaks, hornbeams and birches. The forest offers the hiker more than 1,200 miles of roads and footpaths.

Less well-known and not far from there is the castle of Vaux-le-Vicomte, built by Le Vau for Fouquet, Louis XIV's finance minister. But the ostentatious

display angered the sovereign and the castle's over-ambitious owner ended his days in prison.

Although it is a private estate, Vaux is nevertheless open to visitors and provides a marvelous picture of seignorial life in Louis XIV's time.

To the north, Chantilly, built by Connetable de Montmorency, today houses a rich museum of paintings, ceramics, manuscripts and, in particular, Jean Fouquet's valuable miniatures. Annexes, gardens, the park... And all around, the forest of Chantilly extending to the estates of Ermenonville, and Mortefontaine with its romantic ponds and old towns like Senlis and small rural towns lost at the edge of Valois, still so rich in local traditions.

Further north, Compiègne adjoins the forest of Villers-Cotterêts. It is a late 18th century royal palace containing chiefly mementos of Napoleon III and his Court. Memorable celebrations took place there; still today, on rare occasions, there is hunting in the neighboring forest.

There is no scarcity of castles in the west. Near the forest of Dreux is Anet, a model of graceful architecture that Philibert of Orme built for Diana of Poitiers, the favorite of Henry II.

Further south are Dreux and its royal chapel and Chartres and its wonderful cathedral, the most beautiful poem in stone ever created by French art. Further east is Rambouillet and its castle, the presidential residence.

From Pontchartrain to Neauphle-le-Château, from Maintenon, and further south to Courance, built in a beautiful Louis XIII style, there are few places without their castle, their towers and their ruins.

The Seine Valley

It is as well to consider the Seine Valley—downstream from Paris—along with the Parisian Basin, for the Seine links Paris to the ocean. Another reason for taking the two together is that ambitious plans for the year 2000 provide for the extension of the Parisian agglomeration along this Valley to the Channel.

Everything leads there: the river, the railways, the highways and soon the new cities—such as Cery near Pontoise or Corbeil—will blaze the trail for this gigantic aggregation.

While there is still time let us enjoy the charm of the Valley whose countryside of fields and streams, of forests and castles maintains the characteristics of the Ile-de-France and often also its history.

From Mantes to Rouen.

Mantes is the first stop. It is called Mantes-la-Jolie and undoubtedly it deserves to be called lovely. The towers of the cathedral are reflected in the waters of the river. Largely built at the beginning of the 13th century, it is one of the purest examples of early Gothic art. The nave rises more than 100 feet in the limpid elegance of its six bays.

Already castles can be seen rising on the steep slopes and chalky cliffs: Roche Guyon where Lamartine lived... Valleys open up whose streams, such as the Epte with its clear waters, swell the Seine. Old cities come into view amid the green countryside: Vernon, Gaillon with its ruined castle and the Andelys very close to the Château Gaillard. The castle is nothing but ruins, but its proud silhouette dominates the valley and gives an impressive idea of what a fortified castle was like in the Middle Ages.

The plateau which runs along the river finally slopes downward towards the panorama of Rouen with its river port, its ships, its steeples, its towers and its picturesque old districts, devastated during the last war.

Capital of Upper Normandy, Rouen was a land of battles from the time the Normans, the men from the North, came to settle on its banks. It was there that Joan of Arc perished at the stake for having restored the "noble country of France" to its king. Today Rouen is a big industrial city and a commercial outlet towards the northern countries.

Monuments have been restored: the cathedral which in the 15th century adorned itself in the exuberance of flamboyant Gothic, the Big Clock of the 16th century, the belfrey, the Bourgtheroulde mansion where the flamboyant and the Renaissance styles blend, Saint-Maclou with its cloister, the law courts, Saint-Ouen! So many architectural treasures make Rouen a museum-city.

From Rouen to the sea.

Beyond Rouen, the Seine continues its winding path between the lands of Caux on the right and Auge on the left. Other marvels on its banks are the Abbey of Jumièges, founded in the 7th century and at one time the Vikings' headquarters; Saint-Wandrille, a partially ruined Benedictine abbey; Caudebec-en-Caux and its old dwellings; Tancarville with its avant-garde bridge; and lastly the strange lands of the Marais Vernier just before the estuary of the Seine.

Le Havre to the north and Deauville-Trouville to the south mark the boundaries of this estuary, deservedly renowned for the beauty of its skies. Artists settled in Honfleur and on the Côte de Grâce in such numbers that they formed a kind of school there: Boudin and Jongkind were the masters. Honfleur's charming little port with its old houses and big roofs is always enchanting to the eye.

Now we have reached the Channel where modern life takes over. Almost entirely reconstructed after the war, Le Havre is one of the big French ports serving America. To the south are the elegant beaches of Trouville, Deauville, Houlgate and Cabourg which, year after year, take turns being the "in" place, where the "smart set" from Paris and elsewhere meet during the summer months.

Contrasting with this flat coast are Upper Normandy's chalky cliffs to the north of Le Havre: Etretat, Fécamp, Saint-Valéry, Dieppe, Tréport... Family beaches at the foot of hills where lie the fertile lands of Caux and Bray.

Left: The Seine at Château-Gaillard. Above: Interior of a Romanesque church on the Ile-de-France.

23

Versailles: Main entrance and courtyard of the Palace.
General view of Palace. The gardens: The Latone basin
and the "green carpet". Right: The castle of Anet.

Those castles that surround Paris, those forests touched by autumn and those ponds and rivers bathed in gentle mist—of how many idylls and passions down the ages have they been the discreet witnesses?

Henry II and Diane of Poitiers at Anet, Louis XIV and Madame de Montespan, Louis XV and La Pompadour at Versailles, Napoléon and Joséphine at Malmaison and Napoléon III and Eugénie at Compiègne. In these great houses kings and emperors lived and loved.

But poets too have left the memory of their loves or dreams on the hillsides and the plains of Ile-de-France. Along the paths of Valois Gérard de Nerval sought the ghost of a Sylvia who was perhaps only a dream. In the woods of Vauboyen to the south of Paris, Victor Hugo and Juliette Drouet lived out their wild love and as soon as they parted, wrote each other passionate letters.

The past lives on in the stones and is present and lingers in the undergrowth. The perfume of the past gives to the countryside of this Ile-de-France something more than the beauty of sky and foliage, something like a subtle emanation from the souls of those long since dead.

Louis IX (Saint Louis). Louis XIV. N^ooléon I.

Some Great Figures down through the Centuries

If Paris is the heart of France, it is also its soul and its spirit. Continually enriched by the contribution of the provinces where ancestral virtues live on, Paris irresistibly excites talent and ambition! There is almost no example of a person destined for greatness who has not at some moment in his career come in contact with this beacon of light.

All the great men of France have left their mark on the walls of the capital.

Clovis, the traditional founder of the Frankish kingdom, died in Paris in the 6th century. After having conquered the country from the Rhine to the Pyrenees, Clovis, the Christian king, settled in Paris.

A century later Dagobert reconstituted the divided kingdom. He was born in Saint-Denis where he founded the Abbey in which his ashes rest. There too were placed the ashes of the kings of France, later to be scattered during the fury of the Revolution.

Charlemagne—Carolus Magnus—the first great conqueror king made of his kingdom an empire which included Saxony, Bavaria, Lombardy and Catalonia. He had it proclaimed the Empire of the West by receiving the crown from the hands of the Pope in the year 800.

"The Emperor with the white flowing beard" made Aix-la-Chapelle his capital. Aix-la-Chapelle, now Aachen, lies outside of France. The empire collapsed with his sons and grandsons and France withdrew within boundaries that were soon to be disputed by the great feudal lords and turbulent neighbors.

It was in Paris that Louis IX signed a treaty with England consolidating the territory. A splendid figure who was canonized, Louis IX (1214-1270) added to the beauty of the capital by building the Sainte-Chapelle and the Sorbonne. During a crusade he died of the plague in Tunisia, but not before he had reformed the system of justice in France.

Two centuries later a young girl saved France from the English invaders. The story of Joan of Arc is unique in the annals of the world. A little Lorraine peasant girl, summoned by celestial voices to "save the kingdom of France", she armed a company of soldiers, went to find the king, placed herself at the head of the army and set towns and castles free. Although she fought in the name of Christ, she died at the stake betrayed to her enemies by the Church and condemned as a heretic.

From the Renaissance to the age of Louis XIV, from the good king Henry IV (nicknamed "Gay Spark" because of his amorous ardor) to the knight king Francis I and the "Sun King", Louis XIV, to the battles and conquests —the most tangible and noble traces of these monarchs' reigns are to be found in the monuments they left. They made France and formed it and if their ostentation sometimes shocks us the future absolves them because they worked for France.

After this triumph came the drama: the people hurled themselves at the castles and the last king, Louis XVI, paid with his life for the extravagance of his ancestors. The guillotine was set up, there were hangings and drownings. There were the grim faces of Mirabeau, Danton and Robespierre.

The freedom that came was dearly bought in the course of this painful birth of a new world.

After that "Napoleon's epic", magnified by popular imagery, could only be an interlude, more dramatic than necessary.

The French Revolution gave the "rights of man" to the world, but it took a century of fragile kingships and a short-lived empire before those rights came alive again in the land which gave birth to them.

Portrait of Molière.

Writers and Poets (1)

In the course of the Middle Ages, the "medieval verse chronicle"—epics of valiant deeds, often more legendary than historical—told the people of the battles of Roland, Charlemagne's valiant knight, the adventures of the Knights of the Round Table and the search for The Holy Grail. At the same time poets and musicians went from castle to castle telling of the joys of courtly love.

In the 15th century, the French language took shape in the works of Villon and Charles d'Orléans. François Villon was the first of the Parisian poets, a disreputable fellow and a true poet.

The Mystery Plays, made famous by Arnould Greban and Pierre Gringore, and given on the square in front of the cathedrals, were a first attempt at theater.

And then the Renaissance exploded with great names which we find as we travel through the country, for the Court and the intellectuals moved in part towards the Loire Valley where the stars of Ronsard and du Bellay shone.

After the verve of Rabelais, the language became more refined and the ideas clearer with the wise Montaigne, scholar and philosopher who lived in a castle in the Périgord.

Court life in the 17th century led to affectation, but in 1634 the French Academy was created, so that the language might be codified and rules given to the literary art.

Among so many fine wits and different talents there are several names of special brilliance. In the world of ideas Descartes' *Discourse on Method* (1637), Pascal's *Pensées* (1670), La Bruyère's *Characters* (1688), La Fontaine's *Fables,* Bossuet's *Sermons,* Perrault's *Popular Tales,* Madame de Sévigné's *Letters* and Boileau's *Poetic Art* mark this classical period.

But it is perhaps in the theater that the French classical period produced its finest, and also most lasting works since today they still retain all their savor and pungency.

Themes from ancient times are the basis of Corneille's and Racine's works, but those themes are merely a pretext for the expression of conflicts of passion and feeling that are part of man's nature regardless of time.

Le Cid, Horace and *Polyeucte* mark the zenith of Corneille's dramatic art; *Andromaque, Britannicus, Berenice* and *Phèdre* are Racine's masterpieces. In the second half of the 17th century Molière, going from burlesque farce to the comedy of manners, created an enduring picture of the society of his time and also of man eternal. This is emphasized by the very titles of the plays: *L'Avare, Les Précieuses Ridicules, Le Bourgeois Gentilhomme, Le Malade Imaginaire,* etc.

Writers and Poets (2)

If the 18th century in France is called the Age of Enlightenment it is because it was then that the direction of ideas took shape and was enlarged. The Versailles Court no longer monop-

27

olized the talents of the writers. In Paris, in the neighboring castles—such as Sceaux where the Duchess of Maine reigned supreme—literary *salons* and clubs came into being and those who frequented them used their pens in the service of new philosophical concepts.

Montesquieu wrote *L'Esprit des Lois* (1748), Voltaire *Tolerance* (1753), Jean-Jacques Rousseau *Contrat Social* (1762), and Diderot provided the stimulus for the *Encyclopedia* which brought together the whole of human knowledge.

The critical spirit, the observation of nature, the study of feelings and social problems move from the essay to the novel with the advent of Father Prévost and Bernardin de Saint-Pierre, and to the theater with Marivaux, Beaumarchais and Diderot himself.

Neither the Revolution nor the Empire were to favor the flowering of new ideas. But already in his first novels, *Atala* and *René,* Chateaubriand opened the way for a Romanticism which would flourish during the first half of the 19th century in all the fields of literature.

Madame de Staël, and Stendhal in his first essays, analyzed these modern trends. The triumph of Romanticism in the theater was splendidly sealed by Victor Hugo's *Hernani.*

Romanticism was soon to find its place in poetry, producing some of the greatest names in the history of French poetry: Victor Hugo, the giant, as forceful in legendary epic as he is tender in intimate expression gave us *La Légende des Siècles, Rayons et les Ombres,* and his lyric dramas. Alphonse de Lamartine, politician and poet, wrote *Meditations.* And there were Alfred de Vigny and Alfred de Musset, whose sensitivity was exalted in the worship of pain.

Two great names assert themselves as novelists: Stendhal who denounced hypocrisy, and the extremely prolific Honoré de Balzac, author of that all-embracing and powerful work, *The Human Comedy* which, with the sweep of the artist's brush, takes in every social stratum, every variety and every possible feeling.

During the 19th century, in the field of ideas great historians such as Michelet and philosophers like Auguste Comte came to the fore. There were reformers who sought new foundations for society—Saint-Simon, Fourier and Proudhon.

With Balzac romanticism was already leaning towards a new realism. Flaubert widened the breach with *Madame Bovary* and *L'Education sentimentale* as did the Goncourts, Guy de Maupassant, and finally Emile Zola with his series *Rougon Macquart,* which provided a social and human portrayal of his time. After Baudelaire, the great poet of the century and author of *Fleurs du Mal,* poetry moved towards Symbolism with Mallarmé, Rimbaud and Verlaine.

The 20th century saw the rise of other stars: Péguy, Claudel and Apollinaire in poetry and many names in philosophy (Sartre), the novel (Camus), the theater (Anouilh), all of whom unfailingly maintained the vitality and imagination of the French genius.

Paris: the stained glass windows of the Sainte-Chapelle. Facing page: view of the Louvre and the Pont des Arts.

The Arts

For 15 centuries French art in its different forms of expression has brought into prominence brilliant personalities who have blazed new trails, but in the Dark Ages, when the language itself was being moulded, the first works and first trends were created anonymously.

In the silence of the monasteries, the Holy books were illuminated. In the countryside and the small market-towns France was clothed in a "white robe of churches". Romanesque art was born in Poitou, Burgundy, Auvergne and Saintonge with churches and monasteries whose walls were decorated with frescoes.

But with the ogival style—incorrectly called "Gothic"—French art created a technique in architecture which solved the problem of the vault in the most audacious and magnificent way. First employed on the Ile-de-France, the ogival method radiated across the country and then across all Europe. It created on French soil unequalled masterpieces: the cathedrals of Saint-Denis, Paris, Chartres, Reims, Amiens, Beauvais and countless others which make the beauty of French cities, towns and villages.

Who were the architects? We rarely know; with the sculptors, the stone cutters, the workmen of that time, they are "the builders" who worked for future centuries.

The Painters of the Old Regime

In the field of painting, the first personalities appear only in the 15th century when the work of art abandons wall and parchment for canvas and easel.

Jean Fouquet, although still a man of the Middle Ages, was already a Court painter. An even better Court painter came later, Jean Clouet, a splendid portrait-painter who was in the service of Louis XII and then Francis I.

The position of Court painter soon became official, passing from one to the other. This state of affairs led, with good artists like Le Sueur, Le Brun, Mignard, Largillière, Rigaud and Nattier, to an official and pompous artistic style which little by little lost all aesthetic value.

Nevertheless, some artists still kept, at times even in their court portraits or religious scenes, a sense of realism which saved them from rigidity. This was true of the Le Nain brothers, in their paintings of peasants, and the recently rediscovered George de la Tour. Other, like Poussin and Le Lorrain, went to Italy to seek fresh inspiration. The painter of Richelieu and Port-Royal, Philip de Champaigne has left austere and impressive portraits of monks and nuns.

The 18th century to which the tender and melancholic Watteau gave its greatest brilliance was the century of the "Fêtes Galantes" (gay entertainment). Watteau, like Lancret, Boucher, Greuze and Fragonard who followed him, was already witness of a world dying to the sound of violins and the rhythm of idyllic poems. It was a fragile, condemned world in the midst of which Jean-Pierre Chardin stood out because of the sureness of his specifically pictorial art.

The French classical period came to an end with these painters. In sculpture there were some great names such as Germain Pilon, Jean Goujon, Girardon, Coysevox and Pierre Puget... But it is above all in architecture that French classical art has left immortal works: by the use of both antique and Renaissance elements Le Vau, Claude Perrault, Pierre Lescot, Francis Mansart and Jules Hardouin-Mansard created an architectural art that was purely French in its great precision. At about the same time the architectural conceptions of Le Nôtre renewed the art of landscape gardening.

Several great painters: Quentin La Tour, Chardin.
Renoir painting a portrait of his family.

In Montmartre.

The Golden Age of French Painting

The 19th century is the great period of French painting. The discoveries and achievements of Impressionism constitute a phenomenon as important as was the introduction of the ribbed vault in architecture during the 12th century. Impressionism challenged pictorial art and opened the way to all modern painting. It derived from two different styles: Romanticism, which in reaction against Ingres's academic art had found its masters in Delacroix, Géricault and Chasseriau, and Realism, created by the lesser masters of the beginning of the century, among them the painters of the Valencian school. Later it was to come to flower in the art of the French painters Corot, Millet, Courbet and Theodore Rousseau.

Impressionism is revolutionary at one and the same time on the technical level by the breaking up of color and on the expressive level by the new consciousness that for the painter's eye things are only what they seem. Claude Monet painted the cathedral of Rouen at all hours of the day and the water lilies in his garden in all seasons.

A surprising flowering of genius sprang up simultaneously around these theories, deepening and extending them. It was a genius expressed by Manet, Pissaro, Renoir, Degas, Seurat, who did not form a school but remained individualists. By different means they led French art into as yet untrodden paths. At about the same time the genius of three masters, on whose concepts all 20th century painting is founded, was unfolding: Cezanne, Van Gogh and Gauguin. The 20th century in turn has been marked by the searching and experimenting of other great painters: Picasso, Braque, Matisse and, in abstract art, foreign painters formed in the Parisian School—Juan Gris, Kandinsky.

Left: A village of the Yvelines, only 20 miles from Paris.   Above: The great scientist Lavoisier.   Right: The work of the inspired Eiffel.

Scientists and Research Workers

It is said that the French have an inventive spirit, and indeed, if the history of scientific discoveries and techniques is studied, it is evident that many of the great inventions that condition modern life have often come from the French.

In the 16th century Ambroise Paré blazed a trail which was to lead to modern surgery. Denis Papin discovered the power of steam and in 1707 constructed the first steamboat.

Réaumur studied metals and invented the thermometer which bears his name. Lavoisier analyzed gases and devised the metric system. The Montgolfier brothers tested the first aerostat. Jacquard invented the loom, Chappe the optical telegraph and Garnerin the parachute.

With the 19th century, in France as elsewhere, came a general advance in the sciences as well as many new inventions. But the French often have more imagination than practical sense and a good number of their discoveries are exploited by others. We owe quinine to the work of Pelletier and Caventon. Séguin designed the first suspension bridge. Arago worked on sound and electromagnetism, while Ampère was the father of electro-dynamics. In 1827 Nicéphore Niepce made the first photograph and Daguerre carried on his work which, with that of Janssen, Marey and others, made it possible for Louis Lumière to build the first practical projector for motion pictures in 1895. It was called the cinematograph. Pasteur studied microbes and found a vaccine against rabies.

Edward Branly was one of the moving spirits in the development of wireless telegraphy. Pierre and Marie Curie discovered radium and Calmette the vaccine against tuberculosis.

In the world of automobiles Panhard and Levassor built the first car to use gasoline, and in 1897, while in the aviation field, Ader succeeded in making the first flying machine. Eleven years later Blériot revealed its great possibilities when he crossed the Channel.

In modern construction, the name of Eiffel at least should be mentioned. Immortalized by the tower he built in Paris in 1889, he was responsible for other, no less impressive successes in the erection of metallic structures, particularly the Garabit viaduct in Auvergne (1885). Finally, it should be remembered that the Suez and Panama Canals were due to the initiative of a Frenchman, Ferdinand de Lesseps.

2 - THE NORTHERN AND EASTERN REGIONS

It is in the pages of history that the northern and eastern borderland regions have something in common. Lands that have suffered invasion over the centuries, they bore the final shock of the successive waves of invasion that, throughout time, have pushed peoples from east to west, following the course of the sun.

Last bastion of European defense before the great Atlantic Ocean, these lands have seen and often repulsed the advance of the barbarian hordes from Asia: the Mongols, the Huns, the Visigoths, the Vandals, the Germans and finally the Franks who were to form the kingdom of France from Celtic and Roman Gaul.

But from the time of Charlemagne down to our own day, the same wave was to gather force again and again and drive towards these frontiers, unprotected by natural fortifications, conquerors as well as liberators, stirred up also by French ambitions.

These regions are transit lands and thus have been devastated by wars and ravaged by troops. They are rich in history, continually rising again from the ashes and ruins that have been their lot for so long, but especially these last centuries.

Active and therefore coveted regions, they are more threatened than enriched by modern times! The coal mines and the metallurgical and textile industries which brought prosperity to these regions have lost their place in the sun to the substitute industries. Will their peoples' capacity for work help them over this difficult period and give back to the North and the East their economic potential?

They are also rich lands because of their crops. Wheat, cereals, linen, hemp and beet grow in the flat open plains of the north and of Picardy. Vineyards abound on the well-known hillsides of Champagne and the slopes of the Alsatian mountains. There are wooded lands from the Forest of the Ardennes to the Vosges mountains to the misty horizons where legends are rife and silent rivers flow, sharing the heights of the Argonne. Lands without beauty one might think. But the shores of the North Sea and the canals flanked by rows of poplars have a nostalgic charm sung by poets.

Farther south, from Thierache to the Ardennes and towards the Artois hills and the Somme's humid shores, a subtle mellowness gives promise of that French harmony that is a blend of good sense and equilibrium.

The names of most of the cities, from Dunkirk to Strasbourg, are writ large in history. From the belfries of Flanders and the spires of the cathedrals, the sound of the bells rises into misty skies of the north.

Left: Scenery and atmosphere typical of the Boulogne area. Below: landscape in Alsace.

Vaults of the cathedral of Amiens. Right: View of Meuse and a road in Alsace. The castle of Haut-Koenisberg.

Three Regional Capitals

The north of France is made up of the three provinces of Flanders, Artois and Picardy and in the heart of each there is a large city with a rich historical past: Lille, Arras, Amiens.

They are active, modern cities which, in spite of the devastation of war, still retain monuments of great interest. There are several old, often restored, churches in Lille, the old Stock Exchange in brick and stone, dating from the 17th century, the Rihour palace, a 15th century residence, and the Citadel built by Vauban, the master of French military architecture in Louis XIV's reign. Lille also has a very beautiful Art Museum, particularly rich in Flemish and Dutch paintings.

The capital city of Artois is Arras, so often destroyed down the centuries: by the Normans, by Louis XI; taken from the Spanish in 1640, plundered during the Revolution, bombarded from 1914 to 1918, and again in 1940 and 1944. But Arras has risen again. Its monuments have been restored and the city still has around its main square a number of very fine buildings—the gabled houses, the town hall, the 16th century bell-tower and the cathedral, formerly an abbey and restored after the First World War.

Close to Arras is Notre-Dame de Lorette, built on the Vimy Ridge, with a military cemetery where 34,000 soldiers lie buried.

Finally, Amiens, in the heart of Picardy. The old city has almost disappeared but the splendid cathedral is intact. The latter is one of the finest examples of 13th century Ogival art. There still are old streets near the banks of the Somme offering very beautiful views, and the picturesqueness of the "market on the water" where the market-gardeners bring the produce of their "hortillonages", (gardens crossed by canals upstream from Amiens).

From the Ardennes to the Vosges

To the west of these three northern regions along the coast of the North Sea and the Channel, there are long sandy beaches, interrupted only by the cliffs of Boulonnais and Cape Gris-Nez. Dunkirk, Calais and Boulogne are busy ports. The coast boasts of many seaside resorts, above all those south of Pas-de-Calais, with Le Touquet and Berck-Plage being among the most popular.

To the south of Flanders the flat open country gives way to the first foothills of the Ardennes whose forests and wooded valleys continue to the east towards Charleville-Mézières, Sedan and Verdun along the slopes of Meuse and Argonne.

These too were battlegrounds, marked by four years of hell around the impregnable Verdun.

To the east the fame of the countryside of Champagne is of a happier kind. Badly damaged in 1914, Reims and its cathedral have recovered their splendor. And it is memories of Joan of Arc which the traveler finds most of all.

On the eastern borders, Alsace and Lorraine, partially taken from France in 1871, were restored in 1918, more than half a century ago. Nancy and Strasbourg are also well-known regional capitals, Nancy for the beautiful Place Stanislas, decorated with deservedly famous wrought-iron railings, and Strasbourg for its cathedral of pink

Portrait of Robespierre. The bell-tower of Arras. A small café in Lille. Right: Fields on the plain of Flanders.

sandstone and the old houses with their wooden window bars in the charming section called "Little France".

A rich province, Lorraine has coal and iron mines which have contributed to the growth of the metallurgical industry.

Alsace is made up of two parallel zones: the Vosges region whose rounded mountain peaks known as "ballons" tower over ridges planted with magnificent firs and over the plain between the mountain and the Rhine. Along the Rhine there are picturesque old cities: Colmar, Ribeauvillé, Kayserberg, Sélestat, and, to the south, Mulhouse, an important center. To the north stands Strasbourg asserting its European destiny at the outlet of the dense river and railway traffic from the Northern countries.

Robespierre, Poet and Executioner

Maximilien de Robespierre came from a long line of notaries. Born in Arras on May 6, 1758, he lost his mother when he was seven years old. At the time he was "a gentle, timid and hard-working schoolboy with a passion for keeping birds." After studying in Paris, Robespierre returned to practice law as a member of the Arras Bar. He devoted his free time to a society that was both poetic and pastoral. Having chosen the rose as its symbol, the group called itself the *Rosati*. Director of the Arras Academy, Robespierre became a delegate to the States'-General in 1789.

His peaceful childhood and his literary tastes did not prevent Robespierre from becoming one of the most dreaded leaders of the Revolution and instigator of the justly-named "Reign of Terror"; in 1794 he died on the scaffold like his innumerable victims.

Watteau, Painter of the "Fêtes Galantes"

Jean-Antoine Watteau was the greatest French painter of the light-hearted and pleasant 18th century— at least on the basis of paintings which he has left us. After the formal art of the Court painters, the taste for pleasure was translated in painting in the pastoral scenes where love is king.

But to this rather facile charm, Watteau brought a poetic note and, above all, a melancholy deriving more from his nature than from his talent. Did the author of the *Fêtes Galantes* sense that life would become bitter for him?

The Bell-tower, Guardian and Ornament of the City

From the 11th century onwards the name belfry was used to describe communal towers at the top of which an armed man made the rounds night and day. These towers contained the "Bancloque" which was used to summon city officials and citizens to meetings.

Visible from afar in the great expanse of the Northern plains, the bell-tower was the tangible sign of a community's independence. The right to build it was granted to the city's inhabitants with the letters of freedom. Each one did his level best to ensure that the tower would provide an indication of the city's wealth. Among the most beautiful are those of Amiens, Arras, Douai, Béthune, Saint-Quentin and Soissons.

"The genius of our good, strong Flanders rests on sure foundations; it is real and positive, not subtle or unproductive. Plants, men and animals shoot up at will, grow without effort on these lush and fertile lands, uniformly rich in fertilizer, canals and exuberant and super-abundant vegetation. There, bullock and horse grow so big that they could be mistaken for elephants. A woman is as good as a man—and often better. Somewhat thickset, this is a race that is powerful rather than robust, a race with enormous muscular strength.

"Were they so wrong to be proud, those honest Flemish? Stout and uncouth they may have been, but they managed their affairs wonderfully well. Nobody understood trade, industry and agriculture as they did. Nowhere else were good sense and a sense of reality more prominent. Perhaps no people in the Middle Ages better understood the everyday life or knew better how to take positive action or how to tell a story. Only the lands of Champagne and Flanders can compete with Italy in history. Flanders has its Villani in Froissart and its Machiavelli in Commines."

(Jules Michelet.)

Joan, the Maid of Orléans

Legend will have it that Joan of Arc was a modest shepherdess living alone among her sheep until the day that the "voices" called on her to save France. The truth is totally different. "I did the housework. I did not go to the fields to bring in the lambs and the cattle," she declared during her trial.

In fact, although of modest extraction, Joan's parents owned about 50 acres in Domrémy where she was born around 1412.

Educated and intelligent enough to understand France's misfortunes the 16 year old Joan, driven with her family and the villagers from Domrémy by the Burgundian troops, left Neuf-château with a group of friends to join King Charles VII and persuade him to give her a small army in order to "throw the English out of France". She delivered besieged Orléans and had the king crowned in Reims. But she was betrayed, sold to the English and condemned by the Church as a heretic. She died at the stake in Rouen in 1431.

The village of Riquewihr. Below: The famous wrought-iron gateway of Stanislas Place in Nancy. Right: The "smile" of Reims (statue at the central portal of the cathedral).

In one of his books Maurice Barrès, him-self a native of Lorraine, evokes the memory of Joan of Arc: "An hour from Domrémy, off the main road and in the woods near the Saint-Thiébaud fountain, the chapel of Notre-Dame-de-Bermont still stands. Al-most every Saturday the child came and prayed here as she listened to the sound of the church bells.

"It is to this chapel that one must go to be nearest, in spirit, to Joan. I am overcome by respect for the young girls I meet on the road. Joan's shadow lies on this valley, like the shadow of a mysterious moon.

"The fountain has not changed; it is there, amid the hawthorn, wild roses and holly that she loved to pick, to weave into gar-lands and offer to the patron saints of the hermitage, to Saint Anne, Saint John and Saint Thiébaud. Their rugged statues are still there to be consulted and listened to...

"Joan was a great poet who came to this deserted place to receive orders from her voices."

3 - THE LANDS OF THE WEST AND THE LOIRE VALLEY

In the ever-difficult task of dividing up the "hexagon", as France is sometimes called because of its shape, it is the climate that guides us more than the provinces or even ethnic characteristics. Thus the entire western part of the country, from the Seine Estuary to that of the Garonne, is subject to the maritime influences of the Atlantic.

The fertile lands of lower Normandy, Brittany's heaths and forests, the lands of Poitou and Vendée and the humid valleys of Touraine and Saintonge receive the rainy currents and the maritime winds from the open sea before these strike against the first mountains of the Morvan and the central plateau.

Facing the ocean, these western regions have given France generations of sailors, pirates and explorers. Most of the great captains and pioneers of other continents were born on these lands, particularly in Normandy, a province created by the descendants of the Vikings, and in Saintonge. Cavelier de la Salle, Jacques Cartier and Samuel de Champlain are some of the famous names that we encounter here.

In the center is Brittany, an old Celtic land, long hostile to the Frankish invaders and the last stronghold of French royalty. It is the home base for faraway fishing in Iceland, Newfoundland and Mauritania, and a land of sailors and navigators who by this very fact are all the more attached to their native soil and traditions.

Here are rocky wild coastlines, dotted with islands and buffeted by the winds... Lands of granite where the menhirs (raised stones that have come from the beginning of time) and the Stations of the Cross send up their mute prayer to the tempest torn skies...

It is a region which has kept its faith, its "pilgrimages" and often even the costumes and white headdresses of the womenfolk.

But beyond the harshness of the coastal wastes are the closed valleys and the forests still haunted by the memory of Merlin, the magician, and Vivian, the fairy. Here there is a certain gentleness which is a prelude to that sung by Du Bellay in his native Anjou.

Between the Seine and the Garonne is the Loire, that supremely French river which reflects the happy hills and the gentle sky of Touraine, Blésois and Orléanais. Here is the "royal road" of the art of living, marked out with castles which make its reputation and its glory. Where so many great names in history, literature and the arts have left some link, some memory, there is that harmony which makes the Loire Valley like the Seine Valley the heart of historic France.

The lazily-flowing river is dotted with islands and patches of light-colored sand between its banks of green foliage.

Here we meet ghosts of the past at the river bends and in the avenues of those parks whose beautiful classical landscaping extends to the water's edge. There are the princesses and the favorites, the ostentatious display of Francis I, the shade of Leonardo da Vinci, the cavalcade with Joan the "Maid of Orléans" and those imaginary figures from the pen of Balzac, their memory more substantial than that of people who really lived.

Green fields in Normandy and an old mill in Brittany.

The cathedral of Chartres towering above the corn fields.

Two Sisters with Different Features

The name lower Normandy (as distinct from upper Normandy, discussed in the section on the "Valley of the Seine") is given to that part of the province which extends from the banks of the Dives, that is to say from the Auge valley to the boundaries of Brittany. It is a cattle raising land with plentiful prairies, cut by hedges which mark off the rural plots of land and form the "woodland of Normandy" in the hollows of the small valleys.

At the edge of the Channel stretch the beaches made famous by the Allied invasion in 1944, and at the province's outlet towards the sea there are two cities, Caen and Cherbourg. Some nine miles from the coast, Caen is a river port which has risen from its ruins. It has two magnificent examples of 12th century Norman Romanesque

art: Abbaye-aux-Hommes, the church of St.Etienne and Abbaye-aux-Dames, the church of the Trinity. Cherbourg, a military port with a naval dockyard and a shipbuilding industry, is located to the north of the Contentin Peninsula which is itself rich in architectural remains, at Bayeux, Saint-Lo, Coutances. The finest is the unique and well-preserved Abbey of Mont-Saint-Michel, one of the most visited sites in France. The bay of Mont-Saint-Michel marks the border between Normandy and Brittany. Beyond begins the land of the menhirs and the dolemens, stones erected by the Celts. These stones are particularly numerous in Carnac and Amaret. But the traveler is fascinated even more by the innumerable Stations of the Cross which are frequently found on Brittany's coast and heaths. Hewn in granite and conjuring up the scenes of

the Passion with the poetry and ruggedness of primitive art, these Stations of the Cross constitute genuine Bibles in stone. They should be visited in Guimilian, Pleyben and Saint-Thégonnec, witnesses to an age-old, eternal faith. Gothic art inspired the construction of the cathedrals with slender spires like those of Saint-Pol-de-Léon and Quimper. Alternating with these cathedrals are solid chapels, built to withstand the storms.

Rennes is the capital of Brittany. The two cities of Rennes and Brest— the harbor bastion at the end of a very well-protected bay — form the boundaries of the ancient land of Armorica. The picturesque old ports, the coast battered by the winds, the wild heaths and forests make Brittany one of the most exciting regions of France.

Old shop in Rouen. Side door of the church of Nogent-le-Rotrou. South façade of the church of Notre-Dame in Louviers.

Beaches to Remember

Utah, Omaha, Gold, Juno, Sword...
For the Allies, these five names evoke
the feverish hours of the Normandy
landing. These names, easy to remem-
ber for the young soldiers from across
the Atlantic, had been chosen by the
Military High Command as names
for the beaches bordering the Channel.
Once the storm had passed, Grand-
champ, Vierville, Arromanches, and
Lions-sur-Mer rediscovered their original purpose, that of tranquil summer
resorts. All that remains are the
memory of the landing, faithfully
preserved in an interesting museum,
and the fields of white crosses stretch-
ing as far as the eye can seen in the
green Norman countryside...

Mont-Saint-Michel, « Marvel of the West »

Visible from afar in the vast bay
which surrounds it, the pyramidal mass
of the Cathedral of Mont-Saint-Michel
(begun in the 11th century) rises 260
feet above sea level. The perimeter
of the small island on which this
splendid basilica stands is of more than
2,900 feet. The ebb and flow of the
tides is more perceptible here than
anywhere else, and the difference
between high and low tide can be as
much as 46 feet.

After having admired this fine cathedral and the view offered from the
platform of the Western provinces, the
tourist should be very careful if he
wants to walk upon the sands of the
bay. To the danger of the quick sands,
very general in this area, is added that
of the tide which, it is said, can come
in with the speed of a galloping horse.

46

The great novelist Guy de Maupassant has left us this fine description of Mont-Saint-Michel: "An unimaginable expanse of sand was merging in the distance with sea and sky. A river was flowing there and under the sun-drenched azure sky, it was dotted with luminous patches of water, like holes opening on to another, inner sky... Seven or eight miles off shore, in the midst of this yellow desert still wet from the receding tide, there rose from the sands a monumental profile of angular rock. At the summit of this fantastic pyramid stood a cathedral.

"Further on, in the blue line of the waves, could be seen the brown tips of other sunken rocks. Continuing its tour of the horizon towards the right, the eye picked out, next to this solitude of sand, the vast green expanses of the Normandy countryside, so thickly wooded as to seem like one unending forest. Here was all the wealth of nature at one time and in one place, gathered together in its grandeur and its power, its freshness and its grace. From this vision of forests my gaze passed to the granite mountain, solitary inhabitant of the sands, whose strange Gothic outline was projected on the infinite shore."

47

*Pictures of Brittany: Pen'March,
Trech point, the port of Piriac.*

The Last Bastion of the Druids

For centuries, legends and mysticism have harmonized perfectly on the moors of Brittany. In the first milleniums, the Celts came to Armorica and established the druidic cult. The druids who were priests, sorcerers and soothsayers at one and the same time especially worshipped trees and water, used magic formulas and signs and attached legends to the megaliths which they considered to be the tombs of their gods, heroes or ancestors. Already those "contracts" concluded between men and mythical personages were being drawn up. They were in existence for a long time before Christianity finally took root in Brittany. This goes far to explain the deep attachment that unites the Bretons to their local saints.

The Arthurian Cycle

Of all the legends to come from the land of Armorica, that of the Knights of the Round Table gave rise to the greatest range of fantastic tales.

According to tradition Joseph of Arimatha left Palestine after having buried Christ, taking, in the Holy Grail, some drops of the divine blood. He then settled in the Brocéliande forest in Brittany where all trace of him and his vase was lost.

In the 6th century, King Arthur and his knights met at a round table — to avoid any question of precedence — and decided to go in search of the Grail. Perceval, the hero with a pure soul, was to find it after many adventures.

49

A very old piece of Celtic sculpture at Vannes. The rows of menhirs at Carnac. Portrait of Duguay-Trouin.

A Land of Legends

In the Brocéliande forest too the memory of Vivian the fairy and Merlin the magician lingers on. Merlin, besotted by his love for Vivian, allowed her to enclose him in a magic circle.

The shadow of two other lovers haunts the Cornwall shores, land of King Mark: Tristan and his Isolde, the fair-haired Irish maiden brought from her country to become the sovereign's wife. The drama is unleashed when Tristan and Isolde inadvertently drink a love potion whose effect is to bind them eternally and make Tristan forget his duty.

Another dramatic tale is that of the destruction of the city of Ys, delivered to the devil by Ahès, the shameless daughter of King Grallon. The sovereign, a pious man, survived, but his daughter whom he threw into the sea by divine command was doomed to wander up and down the Breton coast... Transformed into a siren, she lures sailors to their destruction.

Sailors and Pirates

At all times the men of the western provinces have been wedded to the sea. In the 18th century, especially, great names were inscribed in the history of seafaring.

Champlain, the Frenchman who founded Quebec in 1607, was a traveler and colonizer born in Brouage in the Charente. A native of Rennes, La Motte-Picquet became famous in the war against the English; a Norman, Dumont d'Urville was given the task of finding out what had happened to La Pérouse. Duperre, a native of La Rochelle, stormed Cadiz in 1823 and Algiers 13 years later. Dupetit-Thouars of Saumur died gloriously at the battle of the Nile in the course of Bonaparte's Egyptian expedition. Duguay-Trouin, who was born in Saint-Malo, known as the "city of pirates", seized countless ships, but he always displayed a chivalrous spirit towards his victims.

50

Very old Madonna in its niche in a wall at Locronan. Gulf of Morbihan. The sea at Belle-Ile.

*Opposite: A character-
istic Breton village.*

*Below: Rocks of Bréhat
island.*

Right: Raz Point.

"Nothing is as sinister and terrible as the coast of Brest; it is the uttermost end, the tip, the prow of the old world. Here the two enemies are face to face: earth and sea, man and nature. When nature is roused to a fury, when wave upon towering wave piles up in one gigantic mass... This is a sight that must be seen at Raz Point, that jagged precipice, 650 feet above the sea, which commands a view of the coast for miles around. This we might call the sanctuary of the Celtic world. What you see beyond the *baie des Trépassés* (bay of the dead) is the island of Sein, a melancholy sand bank without trees and almost without shelter. A few poor and compassionate families live there, and year after year they go to the rescue of the shipwrecked. On this island dwelt the sacred virgins who meted out to the Celts good weather or shipwreck. Here they celebrated their sad and deadly orgy; and navigators listened in terror to the clashing of the barbaric cymbals from the open sea. According to tradition, this island is the cradle of Myrddyn, the Merlin of the Middle Ages. His tomb is on the other side of Brittany in the Forest of Broceliande beneath the fatal stone where his Vyvyan bewitched him. All those rocks that you see are sunken cities: Douarnez, Is —the Sodom of Brittany; those two crows who are always flying awkwardly shore-wards, are none other than the souls of King Grallon and his daughter. And those whis-tling sounds which seem to be made by the storm, are the *crierien*, ghosts of the ship-wrecked asking for burial."

(Michelet.)

Continuing along the Loire Valley

Nantes, a great river port, is on Breton soil but it is also an outlet for the provinces of Anjou, Touraine and Orléanais through which the Loire flows.

On the banks of the river from Orléans to Angers, sovereigns and princes have left, like so many boundary stones, the evidence of their grandeur.

The "châteaux of the Loire" are a "must" for those who visit France. Chambord, Blois, Chaumont, Cheverny, Chenonceaux, Amboise, Villandry, Ussé and Azay-le-Rideau are some of the prestigious sites, each of them conjuring up some great name from the country's history, some pleasant or tragic episode in the life of the Court.

Chambord was the creation of Francis I, who in 1539 received Charles V there; young women dressed as Greek divinities scattered flowers under the Emperor's footsteps. Louis XIV stayed at Chambord and Molière wrote many of his plays there, including *Le Bourgeois Gentilhomme.*

Blois evokes the memory of Charles of Orléans, better poet than warrior, of Louis XII and his wife, Anne of Brittany and of Claude of France, the wife of Francis I. Claude was very attached to Blois which the king improved and made more beautiful for her.

But the principal memories evoked by Blois are the assassination of the Duke of Guise (1588) and the captivity of Marie de Medici, banished to the castle by her son, Louis XIII.

The castle of Chaumont overlooks the Loire as does Amboise, famous for the parties given there by Francis I and for the memory of Leonardo da Vinci, called by the king to work on its decoration. But at Amboise, the tragic memory of the Conspiracy tarnishes its glittering past.

There are many, many others charming places in the Valley of the Loire and on the banks of the rivers that flow into the Loire; the Indre has Loches, the Vienne Chinon, the Cher Chenonceaux and the Maine Angers.

Other interesting cities stand out as landmarks along the "royal road": Orléans, Blois, Tours and Saumur which are hospitable and well-known to sight-seer and gastronome alike.

55

Balzac by Rodin. Below: The castle of Saché (now a Balzac museum) in Touraine, where Balzac wrote some of his most famous works.

A native of Tours, Balzac never tired of praising his province's charm, "gay, beautiful, good Touraine". The house at 39 rue Nationale in which Balzac was born could be seen until 1940. The author of the *Human Comedy*—in which he depicts not only Parisian life but also the characters typical of his province—was fond of expatiating on the loveliness of the women there.

"In Touraine you will see many women with beautiful shoulders." And to justify his love of Touraine, Balzac has left this touching confession: "I do not love it as one loves his cradle nor as one loves an oasis in the desert;

I love it as an artist loves Art! Without Touraine, perhaps I could no longer live!"

Rabelais and the house where he was born. Below: Castle of Blois: a door.

The "Garden of France"

Rabelais wrote, "I was born and was nurtured in Touraine, the garden of France."

The author of *Gargantua* spent his childhood in the manor of Devinière, close to Chinon. Rabelais, who was a Benedictine and also a doctor, was a protégé of Cardinal du Bellay. He was very fond of painting his native province in words, and it was a town close to Chinon which he picked as a setting for the dispute between the shepherds that led to the famous Picrocholine war described in *Gargantua*. Ronsard, who was a native of Vendôme, was Rabelais' friend. He was born in 1524 in the feudal manor of the Poissonnière. Ronsard untiringly roamed the countryside "sometimes in a village and sometimes in a forest and sometimes through lonely and out-of-the-way spots" with his friends from *La Pléiade*: du Bellay from Anjou, Baif from Flèche and Rémi Belleau from Nogent.

The philosopher, mathematician and physicist René Descartes, who was born in La Haye-en-Touraine, also enriched the "garden of France".

Francis I, Builder

Francis I's name remains linked with many castles of the Loire Valley: Azay-le-Rideau where he lived, Blois to which he added a magnificent staircase and a wing that was inspired by Vatican architecture, Chenonceaux and Clos-Lucé near Amboise where Leonardo da Vinci died. However, two castles in particular cherish the memory of Francis I: Amboise and Chambord.

It was to Amboise that the six year old Francis of Angoulême came to live with his mother, Louise of Savoy. There he spent his youth, perfected his education and learned of his accession to the throne. After he was crowned he lived there for three more years and organized the brilliant Court life which characterized his reign.

Chambord is the work of the king who had discovered "beauty" in Italy. In spite of his precarious financial situation, Francis I kept construction going and in 1539 received Charles V there. Francis I's guest was amazed by this castle which he considered "the epitome of human ingenuity".

Aerial view of the port of La Rochelle.   Right: The Marais Poitevin.

The Western Provinces

Between the estuaries of the Loire and the Gironde are the regions that may be termed the western provinces, regions with a maritime climate: Vendée and Charente at the edge of the ocean, and behing, Poitou and Angoumois, where we find the first foothills of the central part of the country.

Vendée has two kinds of regions: the Breton marshland, with lowlands where cattle are raised, and woodlands, that are just as rich in pastureland. Further south are the canals of the Poitevin marshland. At the end of the 18th century Vendée was the scene of a counter-revolutionary insurrection which lasted several years.

The towns are not very big. The people of this region live mostly from the sea, from fishing, oyster breeding and from visitors to the seaside resorts. The major resorts of Sables-d'Olonne and Royan are very popular.

The activity of the provinces is centralized in cities like Poitiers and Angoulême. They are also noted for the examples of regional Romanesque architecture. It is in Poitiers that we find the cathedral of Notre-Dame la Grande, with its 12th century façade richly decorated with sculptures. It stands on a promontory overlooking the valley. At Angoulême there is the cathedral of Saint-Pierre. Sometimes in small towns there are other examples of churches and monasteries built in an original style according to the principles of Romanesque art. This applies particularly to the Romanesque churches of Saintonge.

There are many interesting places for the traveler to visit who would like to seek out the less well-known and often better-preserved aspects of the French provinces not included in the usual touristic itineraries: ports like La Rochelle with its old towers, dead cities like Brouage, and islands along the coastline such as Noiremoutier, Yeu with its typical Breton look and Ré and Oléron facing Charente.

58

4 - THE CENTRAL PLATEAU

The term "Central Plateau" reflects a geological unity. In the center of the country dominated by the summits of the "puys" (peaks) and the mountains of Cantal — land of extinct volcanoes and lively valleys — the central plateau is the key to a network of mountains which radiates in different directions. To the north, the hills of Nivernais; to the west those of Limousin and the plateau of Millevaches; to the east the mountain ranges of Vivarais, Lyon and Beaujolais; finally to the south the limestone plateaus and the Lozère mountains which mark the frontier of the Mediterranean world.

This compact disposition makes the central plateau the pivot of the whole of France. Between the north and the south, it marks the boundaries of two climatic zones, something that can be recognized from the vegetation as well as from the shape of the houses and the color of the roofs. The Cevennes mountain range which bounds the plateau on the east constitutes a major watershed. There are two springs on the mountain, separated by some 50 to 100 yards, whose waters will never meet: one flows eastward to the Mediterranean basin, the other westward to join the Atlantic.

The western end of the plateau slopes downward gradually, and receives the abundant rains from the ocean. Creuse, Limousin and Auvergne are humid lands that are crossed by an abundance of rivers.

In the Cantal: the Puy Mary. Right: Countryside in the department of the Loire.

But the diversity of the country around the central mountain mass makes its own profound unity more apparent. Auvergne shares with Brittany the distinction of being the oldest territory in France. Today the basaltic rocks and extinct craters of Auvergne are covered with grazing lands but, despite the changes wrought by time, it retains a kind of wild grandeur which gives to the province its character and attraction.

Winters are long and hard. In the villages, tucked away in the hollows of the small valleys or scattered over the high plateaus between the Dore and the Cantal mountains, lives a population of peasants and artisans whose sons are often forced to go elsewhere to earn a living.

Industries have nevertheless taken root on these poor lands. Clermont-Ferrand is an important industrial center, and the edge of the plateau, cities have kept the regional crafts which made their reputations: crockery in Nevers, porcelain in Limoges, cutlery in Thiers. Everywhere, even in the small mountain towns, crafts endure.

On the Gergovie plateau, the last great chieftain of the Gauls, Vercingetorix, tried to resist Roman domination. Gerbert, Pope in 1000 A.D., was the first to conceive the idea of the Crusades. The central plateau, defended by its natural barriers, has never been used as a transit land for a belligerent and has itself rarely been conquered. Perhaps that is why it has been able to preserve its customs and its countryside. There is very little tourism here, in spite of the thermal and curative springs, but some of these, like the waters of Vichy, have acquired an international reputation.

Remains of the castle of Polignac in the department of the Upper Loire. Right: Figure of Christ, on a road in Auvergne. Latticed window in a village in the Cantal.

"In the Land of Berry"

The waters of the green-banked rivers of Cher, Indre and Creuse flow into the Loire. Up-river the land is sterner. Here are the lovely forests of Châteauroux and Tronçais, the woodland that George Sand called "the black valley" and, in Brenne, the ponds and marshlands which start at the treshold of Sologne.

Berry is an old agricultural province which continues to live from crops and cattle raising. It should be discovered at random along the small roads which crisscross it and in the old towns, many of which have changed very little since the time when George Sand, novelist of country life, placed her heroines in this setting.

The region's industry and commerce is attracted to some of the cities — Châteauroux, Châtre, Issoudun and above all Bourges. This last is the province's capital, already in existence when Caesar was alive. Ever-present here is the memory of Jacques Cœur, the financier whose magnificent palace, still today, with the cathedral of Saint-Etienne, is one of the city's main attractions.

Nivernais and Bourbonnais

Situated beyond the Loire, the Nivernais is a region of hills and woods at the foot of the Morvan, but it is the Loire Valley above all that attracts the traveler. Up-river from Orléans several well-known places are to be found along the banks of the Loire: Saint-Benoit-sur-Loire and its famous basilica, Sully-sur-Loire whose imposing castle welcomed Joan of Arc, the Romanesque churches of La Charité and Cosne, the small city of Gien and finally Nevers, built picturesquely on the banks of the Loire. Nevers contains some of the most characteristic examples of French architecture, from the Romanesque church of Saint-Etienne (11th century) to the cathedral of Saint-Cyr and the 15th and 16th century ducal palaces.

Finally higher still, going up the Loire and its tributary the Allier, the traveler reaches the Bourbonnais, where often by chance one comes upon feudal castles like those of Busset, Bourbon-l'Archambault, Roman ruins like those of Néris, old churches like those of Saint-Pierre at Sauvigny and a great number of others.

Moulins is the center of the region; the city has kept its old houses with their corbelling and some very beautiful religious monuments.

Limousin and Its Pasturelands

To the south of the small valleys of Berry and the Bourbonnais the land rises gradually along the hills of the Marche towards the province of Limousin. It is a mysterious area, with its pastures separated by hedges and glades forming tiny enclaves where

sunken roads wind in and out. It is a region of rich vegetation, where all kinds of trees grow, from the oak and the beech to the chestnut tree. Limousin is traversed by cool rivers with lively waters—the Vienne and the Correze. On the river-banks the slate roofed houses are nestled together in the old market towns.

Limoges is the industrial capital of these cattle raising lands. Ten thousand workers are employed in the porcelain industry which has been one of the city's traditional activities since the 18th century. Before that time rural craftsmen were already masters in the art of enameling and making reliquaries and tapestries, for which Aubusson remains a very important center.

From the plateau of Millevaches (about 3,250 feet high) onwards we are in the rude mountain climate. Then comes the Massif Central, true crown of the region. From here the streams and rivers flow to east and west and north and south.

Auvergne, Land of Volcanoes

Clermont-Ferrand, an important city and former capital of Auvergne, is today a busy center of the rubber industry.   Auvergne is also well-known for its health resorts and water-ing-places—Royat, Bourboule and Mont-Dore—and for the skiing slopes of Sancy. But this old volcanic area whose extinct craters stand out along the chain of "puys", has less easily discovered attractions as much from the point of view of nature as of art and the past.

"From the Arverne of Vercingetorix to the Arverne of Pascal", wrote Jean Ajalbert, "from the Gergovia plateau where the Gallic chieftain weakened Caesar's chances, to the summit of the Puy de Dôme several miles away where the future author of *Pensées* was carrying out his famous experiments, how many things there are to move the heart and the spirit for ever!"

With its sturdy, granite churches and its houses of blackish lava, Auver-gne was one of the first centers of Romanesque art.   With their sculpted capitals and low naves, the churches of Notre-Dame of the Port at Clermont and those of Orcival, Issoire, Saint-Nectaire, Brioude and Puy are among the most remarkable examples of 12th century art.   Gothic style is also to be seen in the cathedral of Clermont, at Riom, Saint-Flour and the Chaise-Dieu abbey, in the old Palace of Salers and its fortified surrounding wall.

But Auvergne also deserves attention for its countryside.   The summits of Sancy and the mountains of Cantal rise to almost 6,500 feet.   High plateaus where flocks of sheep and shepherds live tower over the green valleys.

To the east and south, along the mountains of Aubrac and Margeride, the central plateau leans upon the long Cevennes mountain chain which has many fine sites from Velay to the Lozère mountains.   This area is a joy for the traveler eager to discover un-spoilt natural surroundings and cus-toms, still rich in centuries-old tradi-tions.

A Lovely Painting: the Chain of "Puys"

Though her heart belonged to Berry, George Sand, the lady of Nohant, loved above all the central provinces of France.   "It is not Switzerland, it is less awe-inspiring", she wrote.   "It is not Italy, it is more beautiful; it is central France with all its extinct Vesuviuses and covered in splendid vegetation; it is however neither the Auvergne nor the Limousin that you know.   Here there is no rich Limagne, vast and tranquil fields of cereals and prairies in the lee of the distant chain of mountains; no fertile plateaus rising between natural gulches.   No, all is peaks and ravines and the only land that can be farmed lies in the narrow gorges or on steep slopes...

"The view is grandiose.   First come the Cevennes.   In the hazy distance, one can make out the Mezenc with its long slopes and its sudden ravines, behind which rises the Gerbier des Joncs...   There are other mountains, some hemispheric in shape, like the "ballons" of the Vosges, others rising up like sheer walls, their peaks often very jagged.   All around is a vast pano-rama of mountains, covering an area as great as that of the hills around Rome."

Vercingetorix, Mighty Chieftain of the Warriors

No one could have been more aptly named than Vercingetorix from Auvergne ("mighty chieftain of the warriors").

In the year 52 B.C., when he was 20, Vercingetorix and his comrades valiantly withstood the attack against Gergovia led by Caesar and six of his legions (about 30,000 men). Caesar was on the verge of winning when the Gauls discovered the trap he had prepared and forced the Romans to lift their siege a few days later. The Romans left 700 legionaries and 50 centurions on the battlefield.

A short time later, at the end of the siege of Alesia, Vercingetorix was captured and taken to Rome by Caesar. He figured in Caesar's "Triumph"; he was put to death in 46 B.C. after six years in prison.

Gerbert, the Pope of the Year 1000

It was a strange destiny that awaited the peasant boy from Auvergne who was to become the first French Pope. Born near Aurillac, the young boy was noticed, because of his lively intelligence, by monks, who took charge of his education. Gerbert then left for Spain where he attended Arab universities studying medicine and mathematics. Word of Gerbert's fame soon came to the ears of the Emperor Othon who engaged him as his son's tutor.

Elected Pope in 999 under the name of Silvester II, the holy man gave to humanity inventions such as the astrolabe and the first clock with weights. He is said to have introduced Arabic numerals to the West.

Blaise Pascal, a Precocious Genius

Several centuries later, Auvergne saw the flowering of another genius: Blaise Pascal, author of the famous *Pensées.*

Pascal was not satisfied with being exceptionally talented in literature. Already at the age of twelve this young boy born in 1623 in Clermont-Ferrand had surprised his fellow-citizens by his gift for geometry. Four years later he wrote his *Treatise on Conic Sections* which impressed Descartes.

Blaise Pascal proved the weight of air and gave us inventions still appreciated today: a calculating machine and the establishment of "coaches for five centimes" which left at specific times for a fixed itinerary and thus were the forerunners of our buses.

But it is above all by the depth of his philosophical and religious thought that Blaise Pascal dominated his century and found a place in posterity. His *Lettres Provinciales* and even more his *Pensées* are at the pinnacle of intellectual achievement.

Below: Pascal, the most glorious of Auvergne's sons. Right: Characteristic landscape of the Auvergne hills.

66

"As soon as it catches sight of us on the meadow, the wind becomes like a hurricane. At one fell swoop, it ruffles the pools of water between the molehills of black rock. It turns upside down what is left of the big gentian leaves after the wind has torn them from the trees. It attacks us, knocks us about, until we are forced to turn our backs on it. Then for a few seconds, in the last pale light between the clouds sweeping furiously yet slowly in the distance, we gaze upon the lands lying there before us in all their immensity.

"Since this is the country, the buildings are the color of the earth and so the pilgrims' resthouse, the inn, the presbytery and the chapel are almost invisible. Walls are built of the polished blocks that lie scattered in the grass between juniper trees that are half-dead with age. The roofs too are of stone, grey shale with a silken shimmer. Walls and roofs alike are weather-beaten, battered by high winds, torrential rains and heavy snows until they are worn away, as if under the constant rubbing of a thumb. Lichens have made their home there, their grey and golden hues blending so well with the granite and the roofing stones. In this way nature has restored these works of men to its own great setting of plant and mineral."

(Henri Pourrat.)

5 - FROM THE GARONNE TO THE PYRENEES

This part of France, generally termed the South-west, consists of the Aquitaine basin which, from the central plateau and the Pyrenees, feeds the rivers and streams that flow into the Atlantic: the Dordogne, the Lot, the Tarn, the Ariège and the Gers. They join near Bordeaux to form the Gironde, an estuary of the sea cutting deep inland.

Here, at the edge of the Atlantic Ocean, runs a flat coast bordered with ponds and a vast artificial forest, the Landes, which was planted to hold the moving line of the dunes against the menace of the tides.

Such is the general appearance of the region, where there is little relief from the prevailing flatness and the winds from the open sea bring frequent sudden downpours. Its humid climate makes this good farming land and lends a splendid greenness to the Basque countryside on the slopes of the Pyrenees. Further north on the other side of the Garonne, the southern slopes of the Central mountain chain have already a meridional character with often mild winters. It is on the border of the province of Languedoc, where the climate is Mediterranean.

This meeting-place of east and west is also a climatic boundary, though not as abrupt as along the barrier of the Pyrenees, where the two different climates can be appreciated so clearly from the marvelous vantage point formed by the summit of the Rhune on the French-Spanish border.

Here too many chapters of history have been written. As a result of the marriage of Eleanor, the Duke of Aquitaine's daughter, and Henry Plantagenet, heir to the English throne, Aquitaine was long a bone of contention between France and England. The province returned to the French crown in the 15th century.

Its capital, Bordeaux, owes its importance to its maritime position and also to its wine growing industry, source of its wealth.

To the south, all along the Atlantic coast, the forest and the beaches attract tourists. The same is true of the Basque country, with its coastal resorts and its lovely inland villages.

To the east, the mountain chain fills out and rises higher without changing the nature of the landscape. From Pau a veritable festoon of peaks spreads out on the horizon.

Left: The Dordogne valley and the village of Loubressac in the Lot. Below: Picture taken on the banks of the Lot.

Fortified mill in Périgord. Below: View of the St.-Emilion vineyard.

Bordeaux, Gateway to the Ocean

This beautiful city and regional capital, still living a little in its past, was for three centuries from 1154 to 1453 the bridge-head of England, which held the province of Aquitaine. During that time its prosperity increased, then declined until the 18th century. Contacts with the New World then brought about renewed expansion.

From its rich past Bordeaux retains a certain aristocratic nobility, with its old mansions, beautiful squares (Royale, Quinconces and the Gabriel-designed square which houses the Bourse) and avenues like those of Tourny, a place to stroll and meet one's friends.

But alongside these creations of the 18th and 19th centuries are to be found Romanesque and Gothic churches and even, with the Palais Gallien, traces of the Roman occupation.

Closer to our own time, during the wars of the past hundred years Bordeaux was on three occasions the seat of the French government, exiled from Paris: 1870, 1914 and 1940.

It is a business city, at the outlet of the rich wine growing region whose produce is appreciated the world over: Graves, Médoc, Sauternes, Saint-Emilion, Pomerol, Loupiac, are only some of the wines of Bordeaux.

The Aquitaine Basin

Cities converge towards the Gironde estuary, fed by the waters of beautiful rivers: the Dordogne, Lot and Tarn flowing from the central plateau, and the Gers and the Ariège coming from

the Pyrenees to meet the Garonne.

From Périgord to Quercy wooded plateaus cut by deep valleys give the region north of Aquitaine an extremely picturesque character; the great traffic routes have scarcely penetrated here and thus the area has been able to retain its character as regards both scenery and habitat.

Perched on the hillsides in the Dordogne valley, there are old towns such as Domme or Beynac. In the valley of the Vézère the point of interest is the famous prehistoric site of Les Eyzies. In the valley of the Lot there are the Padirac gorge and the site of Rocamadour across the wide plains after Causse.

The towns, which have also remained free of population growth, are agricultural centers and markets where there is no lack of signs of the past and culinary specialties: Perigueux with its cathedral, Cahors and its beautiful Valentré bridge—a 14th century masterpiece—Agen on the Garonne and, to the south, Auch on the edge of the Gers whose cathedral's stalls deserve their fame. More modest are towns like Souillac, "the pearl of Quercy", or Sarlat. Even now in the late 20th century they retain their medieval character.

The feudal manor of Boétie is situated near Sarlat. For Aquitaine is also a land of castles too numerous to list. Suffice it to mention three: the castle of Biron, home of Marshal de Biron who was beheaded in 1604 for having plotted against King Henry IV, and the castles of Hautefort and de Salignac, the latter the home of Fénélon, the Archbishop and writer who protested against Louis XIV's rule in his novel *Telemachus*.

The Atlantic coast and the forest of pines in the Landes.

Facing page, above: Very old tombstones in the Basque country.

Facing page, below: Porch of a church in the Basque country.

From the Landes to the Basque country

A vast pine forest in the sands separates Bordeaux from the Pyrenees. The Landes is uncultivated land, often marshy land that has been stabilized by the planting of conifers. The resin yielded by the pine trees is exploited locally. But it is primarily because of the fields of natural gas that the area in and around Lacq has become a big industrial complex in the past few years.

On this stretch of Atlantic coast, between forest and ocean, the bays-particularly the Bay of Arcachon—are very popular and health-giving tourist centers.

Like its namesake and neighbor across the Spanish border, the French Basque country is a special and even an ethnic land with its own language, its "characters" and its traditions. The origin of the Basque language, above all, remains a mystery. Thought to be of Asiatic origin, it has set philologists problems that have still not been solved.

Two neighboring cities deserve attention: Bayonne, a former fortress, and Biarritz, a seaside resort, made fashionable by Eugenia de Montijo, Napoleon III's wife. It was for a time the meeting place of the European aristocracy.

Behind are "countries" overlapping each other: Béarn with its capital Pau, a beautiful city at the foot of the Pyrenees, Navarre and Bigorre, lands of abundant green and streams that are called "mountain-torrents".

The Pyrenees

An old French melody sings the praises of the "Montagnes Pyrénées". Under sky of exceptional brightness the Pyrenees display all their charms to the mountain lover, from green meadows, hamlets and sheepfolds to waterfalls and high mountain lakes in which the snow covered peaks are reflected. Tarbes is the capital of these Atlantic Pyrenees but better known still are: Cauterets because of its sulphuric mineral waters, Lourdes, one of the world's best-known places of religious pilgrimage and Gavarny, a gigantic rocky amphitheater whose cliffs drop sheer to the valley below.

A Cradle of Humanity

In the Valleys of the Dordogne and the Vézère in Périgord are universally known prehistoric sites. The vestiges discovered in the caves of La Madeleine at Tursac have made it possible to place the Magdalenian period of prehistory.

Buried in the caves in the cliffs which border the valleys at Eyzies and Font-de-Gaume, paintings bear witness to the existence of cavemen and especially Cro-Magnon man who has become a kind of "prototype" of humanity's earliest days.

But it is chiefly at Montignac-en-Périgord, in the caves of Lascaux that the most astounding evidence of our ancestors' artistic sense can be admired.

On September 12, 1840, a dog playing with four schoolboys in the countryside suddenly disappeared into a hole. One of the children cleared a way to follow the dog. His three companions did the same and, lighting several matches, the children discovered a room lined with paintings of a marvelous freshness. They were 20 or 30 thousand years old. Such was the discovery of Lascaux, which has been aptly called the "Sistine Chapel of Pre-history".

From Montaigne to Montesquieu

The French moralist and philosopher, whose mind is certainly one of the most representative of his country, was born in 1533 at Saint-Michel-de-Montaigne in a Périgordian castle. Montaigne was pre-eminently a well-balanced man of good sense. He was sceptical but generous, and a lucid thinker who was capable of friendship.

The castle which can be seen at Montaigne to-day is modern, but the tower of the old castle still exists, with its spiral staircase, its chapel and the room in which the philosopher died. In this room the maxims that were closest to his heart are inscribed on the wood of the old beams.

A century and a half later, another philosopher and historian, Montesquieu, was born not far from Saint-Michel-de-Montaigne in the castle of Brède in the Gironde. Montesquieu, author of *L'Esprit des lois* and *Lettres Persanes,* was one of the precursors of the revolutionary ideas of 1789.

He spent a good part of his life at Brède, reading, making notes, writing and taking care of his vineyards without letting this work interrupt his meditations. With its turrets and its dungeon the castle still has a proud look.

Legendary Figures

The Three Musketeers and *Cyrano de Bergerac,* two works that the theater and cinema have made known to the entire world, have also made popular two legendary figures of "French mythology": d'Artagnan and Cyrano.

Irrevérent, enthusiastic and generous characters, with a tendency to brag, they embody the spirit of the French and more particularly that of the Gascons. But their creators, Alexander Dumas and Edmond Rostand, drew the elements of their legend from fact.

D'Artagnan was Charles de Batz-Castelmore and was born around 1610

Portrait of King Henry IV. The Pau castle where he was born. Right: View of St.-Cyr-la-Popie. Night over the Pyrenees. The castle of Brède where Montesquieu lived.

in the mansion of Castelmore in Gers. The king's musketeer and a man whom Mazarin could trust, he had the title, "Count d'Artagnan", and was governor of Lille. He died during the Campaign in Holland.

His three comrades also existed. Athos is still the name of a castle near Sauveterre of Béarn, Porthos was called Isaac de Portau and Aramis was the lay priest of Aramitz.

Cyrano de Bergerac lived at the same time, from 1619 to 1655. Born in Paris, he was a native of Périgord. He published tragi-comedies which expressed audacious views on nature and politics. He also wrote *The Other World,* "a comic history of the moon and the sun".

King Henry IV's Harsh Boyhood

In 1553 Henry, son of Jeanne d'Albret and Antoine de Bourbon, was born in the castle of Pau. Only days before the birth, his mother was fighting at her husband's side in Flanders but she wanted to return to Béarn so that her child could be born in the castle of his forefathers. Nineteen days of riding in a four-wheeled carriage in the dead of winter over impossible roads!

When the boy was born, his grandfather rubbed his lips with garlic and a little local wine.

At a very early age, the boy was sent to the country to live in a castle next to Pau where he was fed stale bread, milk, eggs and cheese like a little peasant-boy. He ran around barefoot and spoke only Gascon, his mother tongue.

The future Henry IV later went to study in Paris but his harsh boyhood had marked him for life. He became the bon vivant, the dashing captain, the "ladies' man" and, above all, the diplomat who was more clever than scrupulous. He won his crown by renouncing Protestantism. He added his province to the kingdom and to satisfy his compatriots' vainglory cunningly described his action thus: "I am giving France to Béarn, not Béarn to France!"

Harvesting the grapes in Bordeaux. Right: Picture taken in the cellars of a famous vineyard.

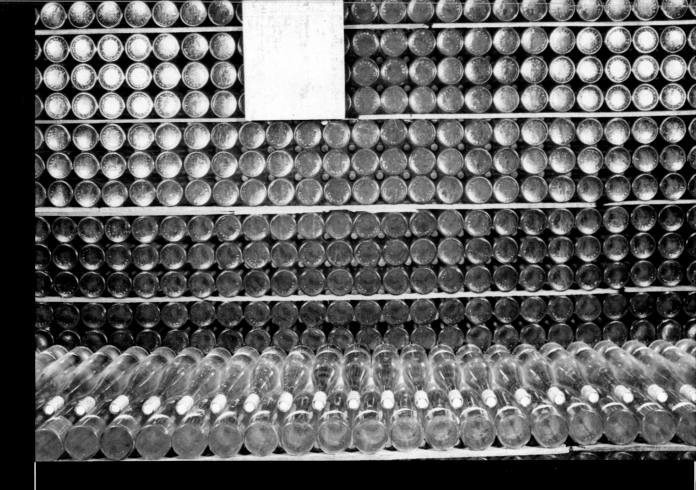

"One evening, the soul of the wine was singing in the bottles," wrote Baudelaire in his famous poem *L'âme du vin,* and the French poet went on to say that it was "a song full of light and brotherhood."

He was talking about the wine of Bordeaux, which is one of France's most prestigious ambassadors. It may safely be said that the whole world looks upon Bordeaux as less a city than a vineyard producing a wine "unrivalled and impossible to plagiarize", as the winegrowers proudly assert!

There are 345,800 acres of a crop which calls for the most meticulous care, especially when it is a question of the great classified wines. For certain of these, the clusters of grapes are examined one by one from the end of September to the beginning of November and picked as they become ripe, a procedure that obliges the winegrowers to stagger their harvests over several months.

These great and internationally famous vineyards are situated on the left bank of the Garonne and the Gironde, in Haut-Médoc, land of the famous "Châteaux": Château-Margaux, Château-Laffitte, Château-Latour, Saint-Estèphe, among others.

Still on the left bank but closer to Bordeaux are to be found the white wines of Cérons and red wines of great renown like Haut-Brion. Finally there is the country of Sauternes with its celebrated Château-Yquem, "king of wines and wine of kings", as the time-honored expression goes.

The winegrowers of Bordeaux also produce wines of a less imposing quality, but they too are outstanding: Saint-Emilion, Pomerol, Entre-Deux-Mers, to name a few.

6 - THE LANGUEDOCIAN MIDI

The Languedocian Midi belongs to the Mediterranean world. The Gulf of the Lions washes the shores of the province from the mouth of the Rhône to Roussillon, but the boundaries of Languedoc extend along the river to beyond Valence.

The mountains—the reverse side of the Cevennes—form here, as in the south, the eastern part of the Pyrenees. They give balance to a climate and a vegetation that are much less meridional than in the lands of Provence located east of the Rhône. Only on the coastal plain, on the gently sloping hills of the Corbières and on certain "garrigues" (stony, sun-drenched hills) of Gard does one find the arid appearance and hard lines of the Mediterranean landscape. As the corridor between Italy and Spain, Languedoc's coastal region played an important role in the development of the Roman Empire. It was used by the Carthaginians and the Arabs to reach the north. In these parts there is no lack of historical associations or of traces of religious struggle over the centuries.

In the center of the Aquitaine basin which joins the Southwestern provinces, Toulouse, its capital city, is on the way to becoming the great metropolis of the Pyrenean south. This is a fertile region, rich in fruits and vegetables, especially in the Garonne valley. The luminous quality of the sky, the scenic beauty, the monuments of the past—churches, abbeys, castles—are in themselves great tourist attractions, but to add to all these, there are the resorts that in our day offer every facility to the winter sports enthusiast.

Left: Languedocian countryside (St.-Guirand, Hérault). Below: Carcassone.

The church of the Dominicans in Toulouse.

Toulouse, City of Past and Future

The Place du Capitole is the heart of Toulouse. Its name derives from the consuls or "capitouls" who governed the city in the Middle Ages under the rule of the noble family Raimond. All roads lead to the Place du Capitole or away from it. It is also at the heart of the old city, between the Saint-Sernin basilica and the Saint-Etienne cathedral, and close to the old sections, so rich in the beautiful mansions that give to Toulouse its charm for the tourist.

But the Place du Capitole draws its animation and its life from the modern city, which extends its tentacles towards the peripheral sections and satellite cities that will make of it tomorrow an urban area of more than 500,000 inhabitants.

Like the other cities of Languedoc Toulouse is a "red city", a city of brick that is weathered by the sun.

The church of Saint-Sernin with its five naves and large transepts is the largest Romanesque church in the South. In it is the tomb of the saint, Toulouse's first bishop, martyred in 250 A.D.

Other churches worthy of the art lover's attention are the unusual Saint-Etienne cathedral, the basilica of Notre-Dame la Daurade and the Dominican church of Notre-Dame du Taur. But the special characteristic of Toulouse is the old mansions to be discovered in the side streets. They offer marvelous examples of 16th and 17th century secular architecture in France. The Assézat, Bernuy, Boysson and Epsie, all of them magnificent Renaissance residences, recall the pomp and splendor of a history which also had its tragic hours in the course of the fierce crusade against the Albigenses, who had been branded as heretics by the Pope.

In the world of modern France, Toulouse is busily engaged in aeronautics. At the end of the 1914-18 war it was in Toulouse that Mermoz and his friends created the "line" which links France to South America. It was in Toulouse that the Concord, fastest plane in the world, was born. Today the city is a major center of French aeronautical construction.

From the Cevennes to the Pyrenees

South of the central plateau, "red" Languedoc is a land of beautiful valleys and of scenery that varies from mountainous to flat. Protected from the north by its barrier of mountains, it is open to meridional influence by virtue of the gap in the mountains provided by the Aude River. Three busy provincial cities in the plains are Montauban, Albi and Castres, all rich in monuments and memories.

Albi is a city to visit with its remarkable Cathedral of Sainte-Cécile, a veritable fortress built on the banks of the River Tarn, and its 260 foot deep dungeon, and the neighboring palace of Berbie whose terraces overlook the river.

Further east towards Gard and Hérault, one is already in the Mediterranean world, and, in Nîmes, in the Roman world. Nîmes has a wealth of Roman remains: the Arena, the Maison Carrée, the Tour Magne, the baths, and not far from there the famous Pont du Gard, a Roman aqueduct, equalled only by the aqueduct in Segovia, Spain.

It is also a pleasure in these green valleys and fertile hills to come upon old towns that seem to have sprung up from the past: Conques in Rourgue, Cordes not far from Albi and Saint Bertrand de Comminges in the central Pyrenees. Here and there the past survives and asserts itself!

Facing page, top: The rocky gorge of the Tarn. Above: The cloister of the Augustinians in Toulouse. Left: The amphitheater in Nîmes.

In the Département of Ariège, on a rocky peak almost 4,000 feet above sea level stand the ruins of the Montségur castle. The tragic events that took place there marked the end of the Albigensian heresy (which maintained that evil was no less absolute than good and that there were two creators, and not just one) and the triumph of the "Albigensian Crusade".

After many decades of bitter fighting, the Albigenses had found a seemingly impregnable refuge at Montségur, thanks to the sympathetic understanding of Ramon de Perella, lord of the manor. But following the murder of the principal members of the Inquisition court at Avignonet, Blanche of Castille ordered that "the head of the dragon be cut off" by the destruction of Montségur.

The siege began in May 1243. For almost a year the attackers, camped at the foot of the cliffs, were unable to move against the castle which was defended by a garrison of some 300 men who had taken refuge there with their families. About 50 of the "Perfect"—the priests of the sect—were also in the castle, together with Ramon de Perella, his family and his servants.

A guide's treachery allowed a group of "crusaders" to infiltrate by night along the southern cliff and to establish themselves about 100 yards from the castle. A mortar brought up a short time later made the situation of the besieged untenable. The surrender terms were the following: "Those heretics and other persons who would not abjure Albigensianism were to be burned at the stake. The others, after having confessed their error, could leave the place with arms and baggage and would be free."

On March 16, 1244, a gigantic stake was set up at the foot of the mountain. Two hundred and ten persons, having refused to abjure their faith, were burnt alive. Among them were many women, including Esclarmonde de Perella, daughter of the Lord of the manor, her mother Corbella and her grandmother, the Marquesia de Lantar.

*Facing page: The village of Montségur.
Left: Porch of the Abbey of Fontfroide
(Aude). Below: St.-Jean-de-Buèges,
a very old Languedocian city.*

Bardon, a village in the department of Hérault. Modern buildings at Grande-Motte on the Languedocian coast of the Mediterranean. Right: Street in a small town in lower Languedoc.

The Languedoc Littoral

The Romans made this region into the province of Narbonne. Cicero called it "The Latin Boulevard". Today it is the land of vineyards on the hills of Corbières; the wines produced in the plain around Béziers are not of the same standard as those of Burgundy or Bordeaux but there are plenty of them and they provide the French with "table wine", the national drink.

Some of the towns in this area are not built directly on the coast, because of the intervening ponds and marshes but back a bit on the first slopes. Three examples are: Montpellier, a university city, Béziers, a wine-growing center and Narbonne, a seaport until the 17th century since when its bay has been blocked little by little by sand.

Finally, one must not fail to see the inland town of Carcassonne where the past is everywhere. It is the most extraordinary example of a feudal city to be seen in France. It has a triple, fortified surrounding wall, a dungeon, turrets, jousting lists, a castle which housed the Counts of Carcassonne, a church... A visit makes it possible to understand what life was like in a medieval city.

Other cities, like Agde and Aigues-Mortes, seem to be asleep between land and water. But bustling on the shores of the Mediterranean is Sète the busy port of the Languedoc coastline. A great deal of fishing is done there. Sète is well-known for its cemetery, that "cemetery of the sea", sung by the poet Paul Valéry. It overlooks the "sea that eternally starts anew"...

Farther south work is going on to turn this coastal region into a modern tourist area.

86

Cerdagne and Roussillon

In the same way that the Atlantic Pyrenees and the Basque country have French and Spanish features, the Mediterranean Pyrenees have two faces: French Roussillon and Spanish Catalonia, both of them Catalan in spirit and customs.

The character of the hinterland itself, in the direction of the Pyrenees of the Ariège towards Bourg-Madame and Ax-les-Thermes, is Spanish to the core. Slopes used for winter sports, mountain streams cascading towards the sea, green valleys which contrast with the arid hills of the littoral, all these are evidence that one is approaching Spain.

Perpignan is the Catalan capital.

For a long time it was part of the kingdom of Aragon and it was not until the 15th century that it surrendered to the king of France after a memorable siege.

Perpignan has retained prestigious monuments testifying to its past: the Castellat fortress, the Loge of the sea, the cathedral Saint-Jean and the palace of the kings of Majorca. It also has beautiful walks which add to the pleasure of the visitor's stay except when the cold north wind, the "tramontana", is blowing across the streets and the squares!

To the south, the hills are covered with vineyards that reach as far as the Spanish border around Banyuls and Collioure, the latter a small fortified port which at one time was important.

Heresies in the Middle Ages

In the Middle Ages Languedoc was the scene of a long and bloody struggle conducted by the Papacy against a heresy that had come from Eastern Europe and been able to take root because of the laxity of ecclesiastical morals.

This doctrine, based on the twofold principle of good and evil, saw in earthly life the work of the devil only, a testing-time over which the spirit had to triumph. Hence the name of "Cathares" (the pure) given to its disciples. They were also called "Albigenses", since the heresy had chiefly flourished in the region of Albi.

After the assassination of the Pope's envoy in 1208, Innocent III excommunicated the Count of Toulouse, accused of favoring the doctrine, and sent an army of zealots under Simon de Montfort to smash the movement. The struggle was terrible and the battle ended only in 1244 when the last Albigenses, who had taken refuge in the almost impregnable citadel of Montségur, were massacred or burnt alive in a nearby field.

Today one can visit the ruins of the castle of Montségur, perched like an eagle's nest on a sheer rock at an altitude of 400 feet.

Some Well-known Museums

Languedoc has several first-class regional museums that all art lovers should visit. First of all, there is the Toulouse-Lautrec museum in Albi, very close to the house in which the painter was born. On display there is the most remarkable collection anywhere of Toulouse-Lautrec's work. Two hundred and eight paintings, 149

water colors and drawings, as well as all of Toulouse-Lautrec's famous posters have given the museum an international reputation. Numerous works by modern French painters complete the collection. Ingres was born in Montauban, where the Ingres museum contains a remarkable choice of paintings and souvenirs of his life, particularly the famous violin which has become proverbial in France in the expression "the violin of Ingres". It proves the attraction of a professional for a field other than that which made him famous.

Finally, the Goya museum in the City Hall of Castres should be visited.

In Montpellier, the Fabre museum bears the name of the art collector who founded it. Rich in works of the Flemish and Italian schools, it is even richer in paintings of the French School of the 18th and 19th centuries, especially those by Greuze, Delacroix and Courbet. Some of Houdon's masterpieces can also be admired there.

The Dialects of the South of France and the Minstrels

In France in the Middle Ages, two forms of the spoken language which were already French could be identified: langue d'*Oil,* the dialect spoken north of the Loire and langue d'*Oc,* the one spoken south of the Loire. These two terms came from the way the natives pronounced the word *oui.*

The creation of the French nation under the predominance of Paris brought about the victory of the langue d'Oil. The langue d'Oc remained the basis of the southern dialects—Gascon, Catalan, Limousin and, above all, Provençal, which was the language of the minstrels of southern France. In Languedoc, in the county of Toulouse, there flourished from the 9th century onwards brilliant "courts of love" made famous by the minstrels.

After the crisis caused by the Albigensian movement, an artistic revival took place in Toulouse. In 1323, seven young poets founded the "Compagnie du Gai-Savoir", whose natural descendant is the Academy of Floral Games, founded in the 17th century by Louis XIV (and still existing today in Toulouse) to keep alive the dialects of southern France.

Abbeys and Cloisters

Architecturally rich, particularly in Romanesque buildings, the Languedoc provinces and Roussillon have abbeys as famous in history as they are remarkable in construction and site. On his way the traveler should not fail to visit Sainte-Marie de Comminges and its cloister, decorated with magnificent 16th century woodwork, and in the Corbières region, Fontfroide Abbey which has been restored but whose cloisters and church go back to the 13th century. Also not to be missed is the fortified church of Saint-Savin with its lantern-steeple and its beautiful Romanesque portal.

South of Prades the Abbey of Saint-Michel-de-Cuxa deserves special mention. It was demolished during the Revolution, and later its cloister was reconstructed in the United States on the banks of the Hudson, by the Metropolitan Museum of Art of New York (1938). The part of the abbey that was not shipped to the U.S. was restored on the spot by the Benedictines and the pre-Romanesque parts excavated.

Finally let us mention, because of its magnificent situation and its cloister, Saint-Martin-du-Canigou in the heart of the Eastern Pyrenees, and the monastery of Elne with its Romanesque and Gothic capitals. The remains of an ancient city remind us that Elne's name comes from Helen, mother of Constantine, the Roman emperor.

The Romanesque Abbey of St.-Martin of Canigou (Roussillon) and landscape of the Eastern Pyrenees.

89

7 - FROM BURGUNDY TO THE DAUPHINÉ

The Lake of Geneva and the Rhone Valley divide these regions into two geographical and economic zones. But, in fact, there are three different areas: Burgundy, land of rich vineyards and old towns with brown-tiled roofs: the Franche-Comté and the Jura with mountains and forests as far as the eye can see; and finally, to the south of the Rhone, the two provinces of Savoy and Dauphiné dominated by the giants of the Alps. The Mont Blanc and a succession of mighty peaks extend until south of Grenoble and Briançon where the northern Alps end. To the south of the Luz and the Croix Haute passes, the valleys begin to open onto the southern sky.

The Jura and the Alps are border-lands, the former facing Switzerland and the latter Italy. Savoy, to the south of the Lake of Geneva, long felt itself more Italian than French. Men are brought together by the similarity of their conditions more than they are separated by mountains.

Lyons, mighty metropolis, is a crossroad which filters the flow from the north towards the south, not only from Paris but by way of Strasbourg and Geneva from the Germanic and Scandinavian countries. This is a busy city, with a wealth of industries of all sorts and surrounded by an area also famous for its textile trade. Saint-Etienne, Tarare, Rive-de-Gier and Roanne are some of the textile towns.

Burgundy, Savoy and the Dauphiné have a rich historical past and for a long time clashed with the power of the kings of France. But what could be more French than those Burgundy valleys with their fields and vineyards, those sun-colored villages, and massive Alps, where the scenery ranks among the most beautiful in Europe.

But Burgundy is also French because of its delectable cuisine. The vine, so dear to Noah, has here assumed the status of a divinity!

Indeed, the pleasures of the table are also a joy for the spirit in the same way that the achievements of the mountain climber are also victories of the intelligence. Like the gastronome, the ardent mountain climber repeats a litany—in his case, Chamonix, Mont Blanc, the Drus, Aiguille Verte, Dent du Requin...

There are many, many attractions to make visitors flock to these regions. There have been illustrious people to praise their charms and divine their secrets, from de Saussure, the mountaineer, to Rousseau, the philosopher, from Stendhal to Lamartine. Here romanticism is in the very landscape and in the reflections of the lakes.

Left: A Burgundy vineyard. Below: View of Lake Annecy.

One of the capitals of the Saulieu basilica. Below: Typical Burgundy roofs. Right: Lyons—old, recent and modern.

A Country of "The Good Life"

Although it is not, in fact, a geographical entity, Burgundy is one of France's most characteristic regions. Its unity comes from its history, its traditions and even its inhabitants' accent, solid and rich as the soil.

Land of the "good life", Burgundy has given its name to the wines of its hills, which explains the position the vine occupies in agriculture and the life of the region.

But it is also a crossroad whose pivot is Dijon, former capital of the dukes of Burgundy. There are old houses, the palace of the dukes and the law courts, dating from the Renaissance, numerous churches—particularly Notre-Dame—that attest to the beauty of Burgundian Romanesque and Gothic art. Dijon is a busy city which also plays an important role in the region's intellectual life.

From Dijon to Beaune stretches a land of celebrated vineyards and large market-towns, faithful to their past.

The monastic orders prospered greatly in Burgundy; they have left magnificent testimony of their faith. Churches and monasteries are numerous, from Vezelay, with its Romanesque basilica, the Madeleine, to Tournus, with the church of Saint-Philibert which dates back to the 11th century. Among the monasteries, Cluny, Paray-le-Monial and Fontenay are examples of an art whose influence is found all the way to Sweden and Sicily. Secular architecture is no less well represented, with the buildings already mentioned in Dijon and those of Beaune, whose famous Hôtel-Dieu, founded in 1443, has retained all its original beauty and now houses an excellent museum.

The Highlands

Forming a border with Switzerland, the Jura and the Doubs consist of pasturelands and forests covering the high plateaus. In the past the long and severe winters favored the development of local crafts which grew into industries: in Saint-Cloud pipe making and in Besançon and Morez the manufacture of wooden toys and, in particular, watchmaking.

Located in the hollow of a bend in the Doubs, Besançon is a very old fortified city with a citadel built by Vauban, a beautiful Romano-Gothic cathedral and Renaissance mansions.

On the other side of the large Saône valley, are the lovely forests of Morvan and numerous valleys, now intersected by dams whose construction brought into existence lakes such as those of Settons and Pannecière. Towns are few and far between but there is a famous monastery, Pierre-qui-Vire, a thriving intellectual center.

The Metropolis of Lyons

Midway between Paris and Marseilles, Lyons has always been a "halfway house" crossroads. As such, it was destined to grow in importance.

Founded in 43 B.C. the town was at first established on the Fourvière hill. Under the Emperor Augustus it was the capital of the Roman province, and in the 2nd century already the largest city in Gaul. It soon extended along the banks of the Saône and the Rhône and was annexed to France in 1307.

The Revolution and the White Terror (revolts following the exploitation of the workers in the 19th century) added bloody pages to the city's history.

It was in the 18th century that Italians introduced the silk industry to the region. It was so successful that a century later Lyons was the center of this ever-flourishing industry.

The metallurgical industry, the manu-facture of cutlery and paper and many other industries make Lyons today a city with a population of almost 1,000,000, including the working-class districts of Villeurbanne, Vénissieux, Saint-Fons, etc.

The city has some interesting monuments—the beautiful squares of Bellecour and Terreaux—but it is more a city of work than of tourism. It is often bathed in thick mist from the two big rivers which join there, the Saône and the Rhône.

The textile industries have also developed in Saint-Etienne, Tarare and Roanne, on the western slopes of the Cevennes.

From Lyons, following the wide course of the River Rhone, one passes Vienne on the way to Valence. Valence, a beautiful city and an agricultural market, is the gateway to Provence. It is in the surrounding countryside that the traveler from the north discovers the first olive trees.

In Dijon, capital of Burgundy, is the palace of the Dukes of Burgundy which now houses a museum. Philip the Bold is buried in the Palace. His ambition gave such power to the duchy that in the 15th century it almost destroyed the kingdom of France forever.

His son John, called the "Fearless"— whose reign "began with one murder and ended with another"—was assassinated at Montereau. A century later, when King Francis I was being shown the unfortunate John's skull, his escort said to him, not without reason: "It was through this hole that the English entered France."

John's son, Philip the Good, refused to pay the traditional homage to the King of France and allied himself with the English. "France will die unless a miracle saves her," wrote an historian. The miracle was Joan of Arc.

After his reconciliation with the King of France, Philip the Good continued to enlarge his domain by adding to it, by marriage and inheritance, Brabant, Limburg, Zealand, Holland and Frisia. But all these cities of the North among them Bruges, Gand, Liège,

were full of factions; each year new revolts broke out and then it took battles and rivers of blood before the wealthy burghers, so jealous of their privileges, were subdued. In all these wars, the nobility of the two Burgundies supported the Duke admirably. In order to bind them to him even more closely the Duke had founded, on the occasion of his marriage to Isabella of Portugal, the order of the *Golden Fleece,* which was for a long time the first in Christendom.

But this power had its reverse side! All may have gone well for Philip and his rich vassals but the people were unhappy.

Bands wandered through the provinces living on the peasantry. Only those in the cities were safe; land was tilled only within range of one of the cannons on the ramparts... Famine was so terrible that in Autun the poor ate bread made of a kind of clay; Plague was a commonplace and the sick were dead as soon as they were touched by this scourge.

Finally, after the death of the celebrated Charles the Bold, Burgundy returned to France, though not without a struggle.

Facing page: 18th century staircase in the Palace of the Estates of Burgundy. Left and below: An old café and a view of part of old Lyons.

A valley in the Upper Alps and Mont Aiguille in the Dauphiné.

"These Lofty Mountains..."

All along the Rhone valley, like two gigantic friezes, run the Cevennes mountains on one side and on the other side, more distant and more majestic; the great chain of the Alps. From the Lake of Geneva to the Mediterranean, culminating in Mont Blanc (15,782 feet), the highest peak in Europe, the Alps extend through the two provinces of Savoy and Dauphiné. Savoy was for a long time a duchy linked to Italy or to Sardinia; the Dauphiné was a feudal state ruled by the "Dauphins".

Chambéry, with its castle of the princes of Savoy, and Annecy, with its beautiful lake encircled by mountains, are the main towns in the province. Capital of the Dauphiné is Grenoble, university city on the banks of the Isère, admirably situated at the foot of the great Chartreuse, Belledonne and Oisans mountains. Its courthouse, churches, gardens and museums Fantin-Latour, Stendhal and the Museum of Fine Arts, one of the richest in modern art in France, hold the tourist's attention. It is also a pilot city because of its city planning achievements. Lastly, Grenoble is the starting point for innumerable excursions to the mountains.

The Dauphiné like Savoy is primarily the domain of the alpinist and skier. Summer and winter, the mountains are the main attraction in this area on which the gods have smiled; in the summer there are the ascents of Mont Blanc and the Oisans and in the winter there is skiing on the snow-covered slopes of Mégève, Courchevel, Tignes, Val d'Isère, to name only a few.

Saint Bernard

In the Middle Ages Burgundy was the center of a religious revival which was to have a decisive influence on the history of the Catholic religion.

As early as the 10th century William the Pious, Duke of Aquitaine, founded the monastery of Cluny near Macon. With the Pope's approval it was soon to serve as a pioneer in the task of reforming and renewing the clergy who were then practicing simony.

The Abbey was consecrated in 1095. There remains only one part of the buildings whose conception determined the course of Burgundian Romanesque art and served as a model for religious building throughout Europe.

At the same time Cîteaux, the monastery which gave birth to the Cistercian Order, was founded not far from Dijon. It quickly began to play an important role, spiritually as well as artistically, in the construction of churches and monasteries in an austere style. The monastery at Clairvaux was founded in 1115 by Saint Bernard, a native of Burgundy. It was at Vezelay that he advocated the second Crusade, as the Romanesque part of the famous church of the Madeleine was being finished.

Two Great Names in Literature: Victor Hugo and Lamartine

In France, a literary or artistic career can rarely be pursued other than in Paris; nonetheless, our work and our character often reflect very clearly our native soil.

In 1802 Victor Hugo was born in Besançon, chief city of Franche-Comté. He was, without a doubt, the French writer who enjoyed the most brilliant and most popular acclaim

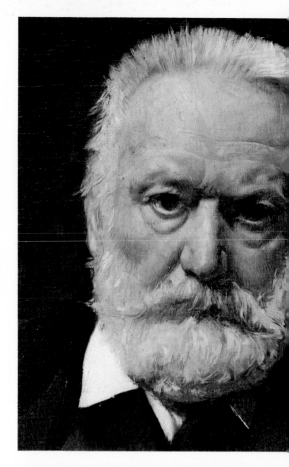

Opposite: Portraits of Victor Hugo and Hector Berlioz. Right: Stendhal and Pasteur.

during his lifetime. His creative genius was extraordinary; poems, essays, tales of travel and dramas in verse flowed from his pen. In 1830, his play *Hernani* marked the triumph of Romanticism on the stage.

In the same year political events changed his social ideas. Profoundly republican and hostile to Napoleon III's government, he was exiled in 1852 and spent almost 20 years in the Channel Islands where he accomplished an great amount of work.

Victor Hugo appears to be a veritable giant of literature, as much because of the breadth of his work as for the flame that animates it... The poet's family home in Besançon houses a Victor Hugo museum.

Another great Romantic poet, Alphonse de Lamartine also played a political role during the 1840's. Born in Macon, his poems sang the praises of Italy where he had spent part of his youth. He lived on the Milly estate in Saint-Point in the Maçonnais.

The poet of unhappy love, Lamartine was for a time a deputy and even a leader of the provisional government, but Louis Napoleon's coup d'état put an end to his political career.

Two Famous Men from the Dauphiné: Stendhal and Berlioz

Stendhal and Berlioz, two great men to whom our century has given their rightful place, spent their youth in Grenoble.

Born in Grenoble, Henri Beyle, later to take the pen name of Stendhal, trained for the diplomatic service, in which he spent his entire career. With his cousin Daru, one of Napoleon's ministers, he traveled in Italy. It was a voyage of discovery—of decisive importance for the young man! He loved Lombardy so much that he had engraved on his tombstone: "Henri Beyle, Milanese!" It was to Milan that he retired after the fall of the Empire, interrupting for a time his political activities. He then began to write essays and travel stories. In 1830 he resumed his profession as a diplomat, living first in Trieste and then in Civita Vecchia. The man of letters was at last revealed by his great novels: *Le Rouge et le Noir, La Chartreuse de Parme* and *Les Chroniques Italiennes.* A subtle analyst of feelings and ambitions, Stendhal is the embodiment of a certain form of French scepticism—egotism. He was not well-known during his lifetime, but today he is considered one of the masters of French prose.

Hector Berlioz spent an austere childhood at La Côte-Saint-André but the discovery of a flute in the attic of his home gave him a taste for music. After having lived for several years in Grenoble, he went to Paris to study medicine, but it was opera that attracted him. In spite of his family's doubts, Berlioz tried his luck at the career of his dreams. He became friendly with the Romanticists and fell in love with an Irish actress, Harriet Smithson. But Paris resented his revolutionary art... His life, like his music, was passionate and powerful. His great works followed one another, *La Damnation de Faust, La Symphonie Fantastique* et the *Requiem.*

By his works, but also by his articles of musical criticism and his grandiose conceptions (he dreamt of ensembles of 3,000 performers!)

Berlioz embodied in France music's romantic genius.

The Precursors of Photography and the Moving Picture: Niepce and Lumière

Near Chalon, on the road from Paris to Lyons, the inscription on a large monument reminds us that "in this village (Saint-Loup-de-Varennes) Nicéphore Niepce invented photography"...

Photography and the moving picture, two inventions that were to revolutionize the modern world, first saw the light of day in this region.

Born in Chalon, Niepce was the first to have the idea of using silver chloride, which becomes black in light. His idea laid the foundations of what was to become photography. In association with Daguerre, he perfected his invention. He died in 1833.

From this invention Antoine Lumière, an artisan from Besançon, created a whole industry—that of photographic plates. It was his sons Auguste and especially Louis who carried to a successful conclusion the incomplete experiments of American inventors (Edison, Muybridge) and others and by so doing made the cinematograph, the first apparatus capable of taking and projecting moving pictures.

The justice of giving to Louis Lumière the title of "inventor of the moving picture" has been argued. But before his apparatus none had yet been perfected, and after him there was nothing essential to be added. Therefore in that sense he can be considered the father of the moving picture.

Pasteur, a Benefactor of Humanity

It would take pages to list the successive discoveries in chemistry and biology which led the scientist Louis Pasteur to his basic work: the system of vaccinations which was to save men from microbic diseases.

Louis Pasteur devoted his life to the study of microbes. For a long time his efforts were contested by his peers, who opposed his research work with their outdated conceptions. He began his work on rabies in 1881 with Doctor Roux, and four years later succeeded in his first experiments, which were destined to save a child who had been bitten by a rabid dog. For the scientist this success was the affirmation of all his endeavors. An institute bearing his name was founded in Paris. The whole of modern life is dependent upon his discoveries, notably in the field of fermentation and medical hygiene.

The Silk Industry in Lyons

After a period of outstanding prosperity in the 15th century, the religious wars and then Louis XIV's wars ruined the fortunes of Lyons, which at the time was a center of international trade. However, Italian craftsmen established themselves in the city to which they introduced the silk industry, thus ensuring the rapid rise of Lyons' trade.

From the end of the 18th century, weavers settled on the slopes of Saint-Paul, Saint-Jean and Croix-Rousse, where they often lived in sordid quarters. With their families, they worked to meet the needs of the silk-traders. The latter installed their stores around the Terreaux and then towards Bellecour. The industry prospered in spite of crises and unbridled competition. Salaries were cut and this led to conflicts with the "canuts" towards the middle of the 19th century. The "canuts"—the weavers, so called from the word "cannette" which is a hollow spool used in weaving—have almost disappeared with the industrialization of the silk trade, and also the partial replacement of silk substitutes and especially artificial silk.

The Izoar Pass and the massif of Mont Blanc. Right: The "Mer de Glace".

With his friend Charles Nodier, Victor Hugo visited the region of Chamonix and the Mont Blanc. Deeply impressed by the magnificence of the glaciers, he described the beauty of a landscape well calculated to arouse the lyricism of his pen.

"At the end of an immense bluish mantle that trails over the slopes of Mont Blanc down to the verdure of Chamonix can be seen the jagged profile of the glacier of Bossons. At first sight its marvelous structure seems both incredible and impossible. Here is surely something more varied and perhaps even more remarkable than that strange Celtic monument of Carnac, whose 3,000 stones, arranged so oddly around the plain, are more than stones yet less than edifices. Picture to yourself prisms of ice—white, green, violet or azure according to which of the sun's rays is falling on them—closely joined together, assuming many different positions, some slanting, some upright, their dazzling cones sharply silhouetted against a dark background of larch trees. It looks like a city of obelisks, pillars, columns and pyramids, a city of temples and tombs, a palace built by fairies for souls and spirits. I am not surprised that the inhabitants of these lands often believe they have seen supernatural beings flying about among the icy spires of this glacier at the hour when the day gives back the glow to the alabaster of their façades and the colors to the mother-of-pearl of their pilasters."

Located on the left bank of the Rhone, the region generally called the "South-east", comprises not only Provence and the two "counties"—Comtat Venaissin and Nice—but also a part of the Dauphiné.

In reality, here again, boundaries were determined by nature rather than by administrative decisions taken by the old or new régime.

The South-east embodies France's presence in the Mediterranean world. Languedoc could also lay claim to this description since it reaches the shores of the Gulf of Lions. But it is only east of the Rhône that the vegetation and the civilization flourish that may be described as peculiar to the land where the olive tree grows.

In the Vieux-Château of Cagnes-sur-Mer there is a particularly interesting regional museum. Several rooms are devoted to the olive tree and its oil. This tree, which Van Gogh said was as beautiful "as a Delacroix", is a symbol of an eternal quality, owing to its long life and the persistence of its foliage, which pays no heed to the cycle of the seasons. Because of fruit and oil, the olive tree also characterizes a common way of life for so many countries and races, from the shores of Provence to the mountains of Kabylia and the lands of Judea!

And everything around the olive tree takes on an identical color: the clarity of the sky, the form of the houses, the appearance of the small ports and those of the villages perched on the hills—even the character of the people. Whether they be Latins, Arabs or Berbers, they have a certain nonchalance which may perhaps be interpreted as an art of living.

It is this world that remains for us to discover, from Valence to Marseilles, from Digne to Menton and on that mountainous island of Corsica, itself a microcosm.

History is present everywhere. Provence like the Narbonnais was the "borderland" of the Roman world. But more than that, it was the first to be touched by the mother civilization of the West, that of Ancient Greece. Marseilles was the "Phocaean city" Massilia, Antibes was Antipolis, and Argèse in Corsica was a Greek town. The image of Greece is still reflected in the silhouette of the landscape and now and then in the women's faces.

Left: The Baux of Provence; cultivated fields in the neighboring plain. Below: The Mediterranean coast at Cassis.

From Valence to La Camargue

The poet of Provence, Frederic Mistral, wrote the *Poème du Rhône.* Other writers after him praised this impetuous and imperial river, which descends in one unbroken sweep from the mists of Lyons to the sea. It is legitimate to say that the Rhone marks the passage from the Nordic to the Mediterranean world. For a long time a traffic of inland water transport existed, often made difficult by floods and the river's caprices. The enormous hydroelectric works carried out in the past twenty years have regulated the course of the river, but its banks have lost a bit of their picturesqueness in the process.

The pilots of the Rhone formed a guild whose traditions go back to medieval and even to Roman times.

Today, the highway, two parallel roads and the railway have replaced the waterway. But the stages of the journey are the same, marked out by towns whose steeples and castles rise on each bank: Bourg Saint-Andéol, Pont Saint-Esprit, Roquemaure, etc.

A little way beyond the river is Montelimar, land of the nougat as La Palud is of the broom. Further south important tourist cities catch the traveler's eye: Orange with its wonderful Roman remains such as the Triumphal Arch and the Theater which go back to Hadrian's reign (each year in the Theater very well-attended performances are given); Avignon, with its encircling ramparts, its Papal Palace-cum-fortress, its churches, its famous ruined bridge on the Rhône and the labyrinth of its streets; finally Arles with its Roman sites, its Arena and Aliscamps, the cemetery with its one remaining avenue of tombs of the pagan Romans.

At this point the Rhône Valley has become a vast cultivated plain which extends to Crau, a wasteland of broken stones, and the Camargue, a sanctuary for wild horses, bulls that are raised for bullfights, and flamingoes. The cultivation of Camargue's rice fields has reduced the space set aside for the aquatic birds. Action has been taken to safeguard the Camargue's character and its animal life. Ponds and endless beaches extend along this coastal zone formed by the Rhône delta.

Provençal Cities

The two big neighboring cities of Marseilles and Aix-en-Provence complement, without resembling, one another.

Marseilles, France's second largest city, with almost 1,000,000 inhabitants, is both an industrial and a commercial center of international importance. This "Gateway to the East" owes its origin to the Greeks, who came from Phocaea around 600 B.C. A new city resulted from the marriage of Protis, leader of the Phocaeans, to Gyptis, daughter of the native king. It was called Massilia and was to become Marseilles. As Carthage's rival it was Rome's ally. But by siding with Pompey against Caesar the city backed the wrong horse and went into a period of decline.

Its rise soon began again, in spite of much struggle; it had to withstand the Saracens who came from the sea and the Lombards who came from beyond the mountains.

Marseilles is the natural outlet towards the Mediterranean countries and beyond towards Africa and the Far East. For the tourist it is a city enlivened by its picturesque Old Port and the spirit of its inhabitants. In its monuments and its museums it has great archeological and artistic wealth.

Fifty miles from Marseilles, Aix-en-Provence too is making rapid strides. In this aristocratic and university city, the great minds of Southern France reigned supreme. From its past grandeur there remains the beautiful design of its squares and avenues with their splendid mansions and their fountains murmuring in the shade of the plane-

trees. The Cours Mirabeau has kept some of its charm with its sidewalk cafés where the events of the day are discussed! Aix-en-Provence still has one of France's most highly regarded universities.

The Southern Alps and the Lands of Provence

The Alps form a homogeneous mountain range but they too are subject to meridional influence. Sometimes the contrast is striking. South of Grenoble, after the Luz-la-Croix-Haute Pass, the sky clears, the snow stops and by way of Digne and Sisteron, the passes of the "Alpine Route" give way to valleys and the countryside becomes Mediterranean in appearance. The fir trees disappear to make way for the pines, pasture land is replaced by scrub and naked rock is exposed on the bare slopes.

A series of mountain chains, parallel to the sea, rises farther south. Here are picturesque regions and towns bathed in the marvelous light of the Midi.

These mountain chains begin east of the Rhone with the imposing Mont Ventoux, and the Luberon—then come the rough ridges of the Alpilles, the chains of Sainte-Baume and the Maures, until finally we reach the bay of Saint-Tropez.

The topography of the hinterland produces an indented coastline cut by "calanques", a kind of Mediterranean fjord with sheer and rugged white, ocher or red cliffs, leaving little space for big ports. Such a port is that of Toulon, famous for its arsenal, where convicts used to work. It lies in the hollow of a bay that lends itself to coastal defense. But apart from Toulon there are only small coves occupied by seafaring towns and pleasant resorts like Cassis and Bandol, Le Lavandou and Saint-Tropez, and even Hyères with its extremely mild climate.

But the real character of the country becomes evident in Upper Provence, in the austere and luminous valleys and plateaus so well described by the novelist Jean Giono. The purity of the line, the outline of the peaks and the cypresses against a sky of glaring blue, the wide plains, on which grow lavender and wild herbs, make this region particularly attractive.

Steep valleys—veritable canyons like Verdon and Artuby—cut the rocky plateaus swept by the wind. Flocks of sheep graze on the sparse grass. At some of these high altitudes it seems that life has kept a kind of Biblical archaism. This is the shepherd's domain. Lower down, on the coast, is the land of the "pescadous", Provençal fishermen.

*Sisteron. Roman vestiges at Glanum near Saint-Rémy-de-Pro-
vence. Right: Typical Provençal bell-tower at Grillon (Vaucluse).*

One of the pleasantest memories of old Provence are the "Courts of Love" at which the minstrels, those poets and ballad-singers, used to perform; the most talented of them were rewarded with a crown of peacock feathers, placed on their heads by young women of noble birth, some of whom naturally fell in love with the laureates. The story is often told of Bérengère des Baux who gave a magic potion to the "idol" of the day. Having survived this ordeal, the handsome minstrel became favorite at another Court, where he indulged in a fresh adventure. Unfortunately, the lady was married and her husband took things very badly. He killed the unlucky minstrel, and opening his body, removed the heart which he then served, prepared with spices, to his unfaithful wife. Such, at times, are the effects of the sun of Provence.

Left: Countryside in the Var. Above: Photo taken in Saint-Tropez.   Right: Olive and mimosa trees.

The Charms of the Côte d'Azur

The Côte d'Azur was once the winter refuge of the aristocrats of all Europe. English lords, Russian princes and Central European noblemen made the reputation of the Côte at the time of the "belle époque" of retinues and the "decline"! In the past half century the "Riviera", as it was called, has been democratized.   Though the winter visitors are still numerous, it is especially in the summer that the Riviera is invaded by crowds of young people, avid for sun and pleasure. For it is here that all this is found—from the best to the worst—from St.-Raphael to Menton, by way of Cannes, Antibes, Nice and Monaco. Golden beaches, pleasure-ports, casinos and promenades, sun and flowers, games and competitions, parades and nightclubs... Everyone finds what he is looking for!

But the Côte d'Azur has other attractions.   No region in France offers in such a small area so many different sites and so many, often contradictory, features.   In spite of persistent excessive construction, the littoral still has many charming beaches dominated by hills which recede or fall sharply at will on to a sea of cobalt blue. Capes planted with pines—Antibes and Cape Ferrat—peaceful bays, islands here and there—Porquerolles and Lerins.   It takes only two hours by car into the hinterland to discover the solitude of nature unspoilt for as far as the eye can see—wooded ridges or bare hills on which are perched villages with walls that have been cracked by the sun.

Farther on towards the Italian border the altitude changes the scenery. The upper valleys of Cians, Vesubie and Aution lead to the snowfields where for several months in the year skiers take over.

Nice is the queen of the Côte. Already Italian in appearance and in color, it became French in 1860. Cannes and its festivals, Antibes and its yachts, Monte Carlo and its casinos and Menton, capital of the lemon, is each a precious ornament in its own way. Every one of these cities deserves a visit!

Left: Cabris. — Opposite:
Saint-Paul-de-Vence and Biot.
Below: Tourrettes-sur-Loup.

*Right and below: Two views of Cannes.
Facing page: In the hinterland of the
Côte-d'Azur, the Valley of Marvels and
the Gorge of Verdon.*

In Cannes there is a statue of the 19th century British statesman, Lord Brougham, commemorating his dominant role in the city's rise to prosperity. A faithful winter visitor to the Côte d'Azur, Lord Brougham went to Nice in 1834, when the Black Death was rampant in Provence.

At that time the River Var marked the boundary with the Sardinian States, which included Nice, and travelers coming from France were quarantined. Lord Brougham was incensed, declaring that he found the decision stupid. Ordering the carriage to be turned round he rode off, swearing to the heavens that he would never again set foot in Nice!

He searched the Côte until he found a spot to his liking. Cannes, facing the islands of Lérins, pleased him even though at that time it was only a fishing village. Lord Brougham settled down in the only inn but the following year he had a villa built and invited some of his compatriots to his new residence. This was the beginning of Cannes'fortune. In little more than a century it became one of the pearls of the French Riviera.

Corsica. Left: The Gulf of Valinco
(Propriano). Below: Bonifacio.

Corsica, Island of Beauty

Corsica, which lies six or seven hours by boat from the continent, is not a continuation of the Côte d'Azur. Its scenery, its climate and its structure differ essentially from those of Provence because of its harsher and wilder character, intensified by the isolation in which Corsica lived for a long time.

The coastline is very varied—at Piana cut into calanques, at Girolata outlined in quasi Polynesian bays. At Sagone and on the east coast there are stretches of broad beaches, while at Bonifacio it rises in sandstone cliffs.

The peaks of Monte Cinto and Monte Rotondo rise to nearly 9,750 feet. There are wild gorges, immense forests of holly oaks, chestnut trees and larches, lost valleys, and villages steeped in legend. From the touristic point of view, Corsica is one of the most beautiful territories of France. Almost every aspect of sea and mountain awaits discovery there.

The capital, Ajaccio, which seems to have been founded by the Greeks, then destroyed by the Saracens, was rebuilt by the Genoese. It belonged in turn to the republic of Genoa and the king of Aragon before being given to France. Napoleon was born in Ajaccio. This is a city of 50,000 inhabitants and a health resort; so favorably situated, it gives access to the island's various regions.

Bastia to the north and Bonifacio to the south are embarkation ports; the first for ships on their way to Nice and Italy, the second for those going to neighboring Sardinia.

But the charm of this island territory can best be relished outside the main cities. On the roads which crisscross Corsica, it is a joy to discover by chance the small ports tucked away in coves, villages clinging to the mountain sides and the harsh, wild beauty of an expanse of scented heath.

The last "bandits of honor" (men who carried on hereditary-family blood-feuds) disappeared several decades ago but tradition dies hard as does an intense feeling of family honor which can still lead to inflexible enmity.

Several Great Figures

Napoleon Bonaparte, native of Ajaccio where he was born on August 15, 1769, is the dominant figure in the history of Corsica. The house in which he was born still stands and in it are the furniture and the belongings that surrounded him in his childhood and youth. For the Corsicans, Napoleon is the object of a veritable cult. In the City Hall there is a museum devoted to him.

His memory is also present in Nice which was the starting point of his famous Italian campaign, in Toulon which he successfully besieged when only 24 years old and in Cannes—Golfe Juan where he disembarked when he returned from Elba on his way to Paris which he reached by forced marches along the Grasse road, now known as the "Route Napoleon".

All the other historic figures of Provence pale before Napoleon's great shadow, so glorious and so fatal.

In the heart of the cities of Provence other names, both grave and gay, rise up from the past: the Italian poet Petrarch lived at Fontaine de Vaucluse; the "good king René" at Tarascon, heir to the kingdom of Naples over which he could not reign; Mirabeau, in Aix, the deputy from the Third Estate who was one of the moving spirits behind the 1789 Revolution; the famous astrologer Nostradamus who was born in Saint-Rémy; and Pierre-

André Suffren of Saint-Tropez, bold sailor and bailiff in the Order of the Knights of Malta. Then there are many saints whose memory is honored during "bravades" (processions) like the one at Saint-Tropez and pilgrimages. The most famous of the pilgrimages is that of Saintes-Maries-de-la-Mer where the Saint Marys and their black servant Sara disembarked miraculously. This pilgrimage takes place in May. On the great day, caravans of gypsies converge on Campagne from all the corners of Europe.

Above: Portrait of Mirabeau.
Right: Statue of Napoleon at Ajaccio.

118

Renoir's house at Cagnes-sur-Mer. Below: Matisse at work, painted by Albert Marquet.

The Poets of Provence

From the far off days of the troubadours, Provence has always inspired poets. The poets of the langue d'oc still exist today with the "felibres", those local scholars who want to keep Provençal poetry alive in the language of their fathers. Mistral remains their undisputed master. The creator of *Mireille* spent his life in the province whose praises he sang so ardently.

Some of the great names in French literature are those of men of Provence. It is often the setting for the works of Emile Zola, who was born in Aix, and of Alphonse Daudet, two of whose works should be mentioned here: *L'Arlésienne,* made famous everywhere by Bizet's music, and *Les Lettres de mon Moulin,* written in the Fontvieille mill which can be visited in the outskirts of Arles.

The last of these great evocators of Provence is Jean Giono who chose to live on his land in Manosque close to the peasants and shepherds.

The Painters of Light

The Mediterranean Midi is a "chosen land" of the post-Impressionist painters of the French school. There is hardly a Provençal city without its souvenir of one of them, that portrays the beauty of forms moulded by the light! Aix-en-Provence is the territory of Cezanne who found in the Sainte-Victoire mountain a subject which he never tired of repeating because of its ever-changing face.

Very close to Cezanne, Monticelli from Marseilles made his palette sing like a harp. In Arles Van Gogh ceaselessly painted swirling worlds, brilliant suns and nature in sudden radiant blossom.

Saint-Tropez was the cradle of "pointillism" with Signac and Cross, and Matisse too before he found his true style. Chagall's home is in Vence; Bonnard died in Le Cannet; Modigliani and Raoul Dufy worked in Nice, Picasso in Vallauris and Fernand Leger in Biot. Here and there the works of these artists are to be found in museums and chapels.

A "pilgrimage" to seek them out makes an absorbing itinerary for the art lover.

Several types of French houses: surely no country has as great a variety as France...

FRENCH GASTRONOMY

Food and the Art of "Eating Well"

Chinese cooking is said to be the most subtle, but it is probably French cuisine that is the richest and most varied. It is one of the aspects of French life (by no means a minor one); each province boasts its specialties, jealously guarded by generations of "chefs".

In the last century, Brillat-Savarin wrote *The Physiology of Taste* and his disciples cling to what the French call "the art of eating well". Subtle taste buds and a delicate palate are needed. It is significant that in French the word *goût* which is the sense of taste also means the ability to perceive the beautiful.

Paris offers the lover of good food the whole gamut of gastronomic pleasures, ranging from the most sumptuous meals in the luxury restaurants of the "chic" sections to the Parisian "bistrots". The bistrots are modest places, often with a regional or a popular character where, for the delight of their friends, the curious love to discover specialties or recipes that have been passed down in great secrecy by word of mouth.

In Paris there are restaurants which specialize in the cuisine of each region. In the capital, they are the ambassadors of provincial gastronomy, for the genius and richly varied quality of French cooking derives from the very fact that it is regional much more than national in character.

From north to south the Frenchman's taste in drinks differs and he finds his pleasure in different dishes, whose preparation and sauces are also very varied. In fact, to place and define French cuisine, we really need to prepare a map of the country.

The Land of the Beer Drinkers

The beer of the North is well known. It suits perfectly the robust cuisine of this region. It is used to "wet" the sauces in such typical Flanders' dishes as *coq à la bière* which calls for very careful preparation. But above all it is the favorite table drink of the Flemish and their neighbors. Being coffee lovers as well, they willingly follow the advice of the celebrated gastronome Grimod de la Reynière who prescribes "a double dose of coffee at the end of the meal", the better to digest the beer.

Champagne: a Witty Wine

If, as claimed by Voltaire, the sparkling wine of Champagne "is the brilliant image of our French people", it is also France's most famous ambassador throughout the world.

In the province whose name this most famous of all wines bears, the vine was already cultivated in ancient times. In the 5th century Saint Rémy, bishop of Reims, honored the wines of Champagne by offering a cup of "holy wine" to Clovis. As for Henry IV, quite an enthusiast on the subject, he did not scorn his title of Lord of Ay, a wine-producing city near Reims.

However, it was not until the 17th century that champagne came into its own, thanks to a monk, Dom Perignon. From 1670, the corks introduced by him began to pop merrily, symbol of hours of gaiety the world over.

Sauerkraut, Glory of Alsace

In Alsace charcuterie (ham and sausage) is queen and the "assiette alsacienne" (cold meat plate) enjoys well-deserved fame, which Strasbourg's delicious foie gras need not begrudge it. It was in the 18th century that a chef called Close, rediscovered the recipe known to the Romans, and perfected it.

However, the most typical Alsatian dish is Strasbourg's famous light sauerkraut. It is served with sausages, bacon, pork chops or ham all cooked in Alsatian white wine. It is relished with a mug of the region's light-flavored beer or one of its wines: Riesling, Traminer, Gewürztraminer, Sylvaner, to mention only the most outstanding of the 139 classified crus (vintages).

Sea-food and Loire Wines

Besides fish and shellfish assured to them because of the sea belt, the western provinces have other celebrated specialties.

In Normandy, there are the *tripes à la mode de Caen;* in Sarthe, the *rillettes du Mans,* presented in heavy earthenware jars.

Brittany excels in the art of making "crêpes". Whether they are plain or made with egg, wheat or buckwheat and served with ham or jam, everybody enjoys them. A bowl of sweet cider goes well with the crêpes, although the Breton cider is considered by some to be inferior to the famous Normandy cider. Charente has its beds of Marennes oysters, the gourmet's delight.

Better than anyone, Rabelais praised the good food of Touraine... where the "reine-claude" plum owes its name to the first wife of François I.

The kitchens of a big Parisian restaurant.

Two great cheeses compete for the cheese lover's favor: port-salut and camembert. As for wines, no need to do more than name them: muscatel from Nantes, rosés of Anjou, wines of Saumur and Chinon, Vouvray, Bourgueil, enhanced by the warm radiance of the cognac!

In the Gastronomes' Paradise

In the world of good living Burgundy deserves a prominent place for the variety of its cuisine, which is both abundant and delicate.

The high standard of the stock-breeding, the abundance of game, the purity of the rivers vouch for the high quality of the food and the imagination of the Burgundian "gourmand and gourmet" does the rest.

The number of specialities is legion.

Need one mention Burgundy's famous "boeuf bourgignon", "coq au vin", or "escargots"?

But above all it is the vineyards—the most prized in France—that have made the glory of Burgundy. Its wines are known the world over: Pommard, Gevrey-Chambertin. In Yonne, the Chablis, in the Nivernais, the Pouilly, in Beaujolais, the Juliénas and the Moulin-à-vent... No soil is finer or richer.

Thus, it was in Burgundy that an Order of Chivalry, the Knights of Tastevin, was created. The Order is dedicated peacefully to the glory of Bacchus. New members are received in ceremonial "rites" at the castle of Clos-Vougeot.

To offset the effects of food that is sometimes too rich, there is Evian—or Vichy—with famous mineral waters to repair gastronomic excesses!

Mountain Flavors

Cheese is made in the mountain lands. The "tomme" of Savoy and above all the gruyère in the Jura and the Alps are well-known. The celebrated "fondue" is made with the latter. The winter sports enthusiast will recall evenings around a steaming casserole when everybody plunges a fork with a piece of bread at the end of it into the bubbling melted cheese. Each forkful is only a mouthful!

In Auvergne there are the Saint-Nectaire and the Cantal, whose flavor blends perfectly with that of the round loaf of wholemeal bread cooked over a wood fire.

The rugged men of these mountain lands need healthy and invigorating dishes—and these the traveler can also enjoy to the full. "Tripoux" and Auvergnat "potée" have a fine reputation.

Languedoc's culinary tradition

The Toulouse region is one of the best known on the French culinary map. The city itself is situated in the heart of a fertile plain where farming and cattle raising flourish. Toulouse is the cradle of *cassoulet,* which has now become so popular all over the country that people have perhaps forgotten its original taste and quality.

Cassoulet is a stew made of sausages, conserve of goose, bacon rind, sausage, kidney beans and tomato sauce. The recipe varies from one city to another but the quality of the dish depends above all on the preparation and the cooking.

Is cassoulet a recent creation? One could imagine so, since it is not listed in the *Grand Dictionnaire de la Cuisine* published by Alexander Dumas last century.

The Languedoc cuisine has other choice specialities to offer, among them the barbel à la Toulousaine, the braised mutton or lamb, potatoes with chopped parsley, the sauce « aux briques », preserves and chicken sauté à la Toulousaine. The confectionery also has its riches, of which crystallized violets are the most tempting example.

Wines from Bordeaux and Truffles from Périgord

In the Bordeaux region, which counts more than 100 famous wines, meals seem to be primarily pretexts for tasting famous wines! Nevertheless, the region has its special dishes, among them the *cèpes à la bordelaise* and the famous truffles of Périgord. Formerly pigs dug up the truffles but now dogs often do it. This underground black mushroom grows in winter, most often at the foot of oaks.

In the Basque country, it is a "must" to taste "piperade", which is made with beaten eggs, green peppers, pimentos, onions and garlic, and served with slices of fried ham.

In Béarn, one should, of course, try the delicious "chicken in the pot" that the good King Henry wanted to see on the table of each of his subjects on Sundays!

The Mediterranean in your Plate

Bouillabaisse, the pride of Marseilles' restaurant owners, is the greatest regional dish of them all. For it to be really excellent, it requires a great variety of fish and especially the "rascasse" (wrasse) found only in the Mediterranean. Little crayfish and crabs are added and mixed with onions, tomatoes, leeks, Provençal herbs and garlic, which is the savor of the Midi. The combination of all these ingredients, when cooked over a brisk fire, is the delight of gourmets!

Before eating this monument of the culinary art, one must have a drink, and what could be better than a "pastis" made from anise... It is this drink that gives the Marseilles fisherman his verve and inspires his "galejades", those far-fetched tales which everyone listens to and no one believes!

Rue Royale in Paris: here is perhaps the world's most famous restaurant. Facing page: Breton children in traditional costume.

124

SHOWS AND ENTERTAINMENT

"Gay Paris"

All kinds of entertainment is to be found in Paris, but the theater takes first place. Traditional and sometimes even experimental works have their place on the stages of the national theaters. The Comédie Française, founded in 1680, in the reign of Louis XIV, the Opera, the lyric stage established in the Garnier Theater which opened in 1875, the Théâtre National Populaire, which under Jean Vilar revolutionized the staging of plays—all these carry on the work of Dullin, Copeau, Jouvet and Baty, the celebrated "coalition" of the years between the two world wars.

The "théâtre de boulevard" (light comedy) still enjoys unfailing success with Feydeau's plays. A particularly appreciated Parisian specialty is the music hall, with its magnificently produced shows that literally live from the glory of their stars: Maurice Chevalier, Mistinguett, Josephine Baker. In the 19th century cabaret was in favor at the time Toulouse-Lautrec was painting La Goulue and Valentin, the acrobat.

Aristide Bruand (1851), using a slang style, introduced political satire to the cabaret. Although this style still exists it has lost some of its popularity to the chanson and the regular performances in the nightclubs, with their girls, their dances, and their striptease.

The "Giants" of the North

The men of the North are avid lovers of the kind of cockfighting in which these birds' Spurs are equipped with sharp blades, but they also enjoy village-festivals or *ducasses*, traditional celebrations dating back a very long time. During these popular festivities there are amazing processions of giants, either walking or borne on floats. In France, Gayant of Douai, who made his appearance after 1530, seems to have been the ancestor of those figures who originated Flanders and who recall the myths and legends of that part of France.

These "giants" measure from 23 to 26 feet and weigh up to 1,100 pounds. In our day the use of duralumin and steel tubing has made them easier to handle. Besides Gayant, the most famous among them are Lydéric and Phynaert in Lille, Martin and Martine in Cambrai and Reuzes in Cassel.

The Legend of the Four Aymon Sons

A medieval verse chronicle of the 13th century which relates the adventures of the sons of the prince of the Ardennes still survives in popular parades.

Several years after their uncle's assassination, on the orders of Charlemagne, the Aymon sons killed the Emperor's nephew. They then fled to the Ardennes forest where they built a fortress. Hunted down, they took refuge with their father, who as a faithful vassal was obliged to send them away. Helped by the magician Maugis, the Aymon sons withstood the siege mounted by Charlemagne's army and finally peace was made.

The "Pilgrimages" of Brittany

Occasions stamped with a sacred and a profane character, the pilgrimages have remained the most important religious celebrations in Brittany.

Though the wearing of splendid regional costumes has now disappeared from daily life, these ceremonies provide and opportunity for admiring the wealth and diversity of the costumes and headdresses of former days. Big parades take place at Sainte-Anne-d'Auray, Sainte-Anne-la-Palud, Saint-Jean-du-Doigt.

In the afternoon there is a long procession of men and women in local costume singing hymns and carrying banners and polychrome wooden statues. Later, at the popular ball, the lucky tourist will perhaps still see some couples dance the gavotte to the accompaniment of the Breton bagpipes.

The "Bourrée": a Dance of Auvergne

Other than the evenings spent around the fireplace with neighbors who were busy spinning wool while they listened to the recital of legends of days gone by, the peasant of Auvergne had only two diversions: the regional fairs and dancing. The "bourrée" is one of the most typical French folk dances. Dancing with unexpected lightness and grace, couples wearing clogs enact the story of the pursuit of a young girl by a "gallant". The cabrette, a sort of bagpipe sister of the Breton biniou, joins with hurdy-gurdy and violin in beating time for this dance which is now being abandoned by the young people in favor of steps introduced from across the Atlantic.

Basque Country Types and Games

The Basque country is distinctive primarily because of the physical characteristics of its inhabitants which the traveler notices immediately! Small, slim and wiry, the Basque has a natural refinement, something that is noticeable even in the peasants. His bearing is lively, he wears sandals with cord soles—one of the country's special crafts—and covers his head with a small beret.

The Basque language, Euskara, is spoken in the whole region; its origin is unknown, but it remains one of the living languages in France and Spain.

Games are an important part of Basque life, particularly the famous "pelota", played with a ball and a wickerwork racket, which is called a "chistera". Basque pelota is a difficult and hard game that is played and watched with equal enthusiasm.

Dancing is also a popular pastime, above all the "fandango" which is danced to the accompaniment of the local instruments, a small flute and a tambourine.

The Clay Figures of Provence

From the beginning of December the people of Provence, all wearing the costumes of former times, await the visitor to the Foire aux Santons in Marseilles, the annual Fair at which clay figures for the Christmas crib are sold. Here for two months, the Provence of days gone by, with its figures of colored clay ranged along the open-air stands, comes to life again in the heart of the city.

The modeling and painting of the figures is a family activity, carried out at home in the evening. As a regional author reminds us, the purpose of this pleasing craft is, in fact, to decorate the Christmas cribs of Provence. The making of these figures developed in the beginning of the 19th century and that is why they are generally dressed in the fashion of that time.

Battle of Flowers in Nice

The blue fields of lavender perfume the hills of Upper Provence. Around Grasse jasmine is widely cultivated. In February the Tanneron hills are golden with flowering mimosa. Antibes and Nice have nurseries where the rose and the carnation bloom... Flowers are the finery of the Côte d'Azur. They are everywhere, on the balconies and in the gardens.

They play their part in every local fête. The "battle of flowers" has made the reputation of the Carnival of Nice. But flowers are also the object of an important export trade and on them is based the perfume industry, whose capital is Grasse. A visit to a perfumery must naturally be part of everyone's stay on the Côte d'Azur.

Above: Reims: The traditional festival in honor of Joan of Arc.
Facing page: dances in Burgundy and Berry.
Next page: Gardens in the French style (Castle of Chantilly).